Table of Contents

Your Ultimate Guide to The Diverticulitis Diet

The digestive system is the most vulnerable organ in the body that is easily bombarded with unhealthy molecules – in the form of food – that can cause inflammation. Diverticulitis, in particular, is a condition that affects the digestive tract or the pouches that line the intestines called diverticula. Under too much pressure or poor digestive health, the diverticula develop weak spots eventually causing them to bulge out called diverticulosis.

Diverticulosis although common among aging individuals, only a small number of individuals with diverticulosis develop into diverticulitis. However, once a person develops diverticulitis, they may also suffer from other conditions and symptoms such as fever, nausea, abdominal pain, bloody bowel, and abscess.

While maybe common in old age, there is still a way to prevent it from developing into diverticulitis by adopting the Diverticulitis Diet.

What Is the Diverticulitis Diet?

Mild cases of diverticulitis are treated with antibiotics but those suffering from severe diverticulitis may have to rest eating by mouth and may adopt a special type of diet until the bleeding and pain subside. The Diverticulitis Diet is a highly recommended diet that can help alleviate acute diverticulitis. Although this diet is supposed to be short-term, it can bring about huge relief among individuals who suffer from diverticulitis. Moreover, it can also be used by people who have a sensitive digestive system.

While the Diverticulitis Diet is designed for people who suffer from diverticulitis, people who suffer from other digestive distress can benefit from the Diverticulitis diet. Moreover, normal healthy individuals who also want to give their digestive tract enough rest can benefit from this diet.

Phases and Foods That You Can Eat

There are two phases in the Diverticulitis Diet – the clear liquid phase and the low carbohydrate phase. These phases are developed to allow the digestive tract enough time to rest. By allowing the digestive tract to rest, symptoms can also subside.

The Clear Liquid Phase

The Diverticulitis diet starts with consuming only clear liquids for a few days. This is to give your digestive system enough rest to be able to recuperate and heal its own. During this phase, you are only allowed to consume clear liquids including broth, fruit juices (pulp-free), ice chips, ice pops (pulp-free), gelatin, water, tea, black coffee. Clear electrolytes can also be consumed during this phase. Again, the purpose of this phase is to lessen the activities of your digestive tract to give it enough time to rest. The clear liquid diet can last from two to three days under normal conditions. Some people, on the other hand, require more time to adapt to the changes in their diet.

The Low Carbohydrate Phase

As soon as you feel better, you can now add low-fiber foods into your diet. Consumption of foods that are rich in fiber is highly discouraged. Although fiber is important in cleaning the digestive tract, it heightens the activities of the digestive tract. The types of low-fiber foods that you can eat under this diet include canned or cooked fruits (without skin and seeds), eggs, fish, poultry, refined wheat bread, fruit and vegetable juice (pulp-free), low-fiber cereals, milk, yogurt, white rice, pasta, and noodles. You can also consume olive oil as it has low anti-inflammatory properties. Vegetables such as yellow squash, zucchini, and pumpkin can also be eaten while following this diet. Green leafy vegetables are also allowed in this diet as well as root crops as long as they do not have any skin on them.

Foods to Avoid

It is important to take note that there are certain types of foods that can increase the flares of diverticulitis. So even if you have already been feeling better following the consumption of foods that have been recommended under the two eating phases of the Diverticulitis Diet, it is still important that you avoid certain foods completely to avoid flare-ups that can make your condition resurface. This section will discuss on the different types of foods that you should avoid if you want to deal with your diverticulitis.

- **High FODMAP foods:** FODMAPs refer to a type of fermentable carbohydrates. Fermentable carbohydrates may be good among people with normal conditions, but they cause too much activity in the digestive tract. Not consuming too many foods containing fermentable carbohydrates can prevent the build-up of too much pressure in the colon. Examples of foods to avoid include fruits like apples, plums, and pears, milk, yogurt, ice cream, all types of fermented foods, beans, cabbages, Brussels sprouts, onions, and garlic.
- **Red processed meat:** Eating a diet high in red and processed meats can increase the risk of developing diverticulitis. Processed meats contain high amounts of preservatives that may cause inflammatory responses within the digestive tract. Make sure that you avoid bacon, ham, sausages, and other types of processed red meats.
- **Sugary and fatty foods:** Standard Western diet contain high amounts of sugar and fat. Foods such as red meats, refined grains, full-fat dairy, and fried foods can trigger flare-ups of diverticulitis.
- **Carbonated drinks:** Carbonated drinks can produce too much gas within the colon that puts the entire organ into a lot of stress. The presence of elevated pressure in the colon caused by excess gas may increase the flare-up of diverticulitis.
- **Other foods:** Other types of foods that can increase the risk of flare-ups of diverticulitis include nuts and most seeds. Although there are not too many studies that have associated nuts with diverticulitis, experts suggest that the tiny particles from nuts and seeds can be lodged within the pouches of the diverticula and eventually causing infection.
- **Alcoholic beverages:** Alcoholic beverages are also discouraged among people who suffer from diverticulitis. Alcohol causes stress in the colon and also attenuates the population of good microflora in the gut.

How Can A High Fiber Diet Reduce the Risk for Diverticulitis?

While the Diverticulitis Diet encourages the consumption of high fiber diet during diverticulitis flare-up, several studies show that regular consumption of foods rich in fiber can reduce the risk for acute diverticulitis. So do not confuse yourself that the Diverticulitis Diet is only about eating low fiber foods for a long time. The low fiber foods recommended during the second phase is highly encouraged for those who have recently been diagnosed with diverticulitis. Once the patient is already feeling better and is back to a normal state, they need to revert to eating a high fiber diet.

It is important to take note that fiber can soften the stool, so it easily passes through the intestines down to the colon. Moreover, fiber can also sweep the colon and remove digested particulars from the walls of the colon.

Through a high fiber diet, the stool passes smoothly and regularly. This reduces the pressure in the digestive system which prevents the formation of diverticula that may eventually develop into diverticulitis. In fact, a doctor will recommend patients with a high fiber diet first if they are found out to have diverticulosis to avoid it from progressing to diverticulitis.

Older studies found that people who consume at least 25 grams of fiber a day can lower the risk for developing the diverticular disease by as much as 41% compared with those who consumed less fiber daily.

On the other hand, studies show that gut microbiota plays a very vital role in preventing diverticular disease. Foods that are rich in fiber can increase the activity as well as the population of good microbiota. High fiber foods are actually prebiotic foods and they feed and provide the right nutrition for probiotic bacteria.

What Happens When You Follow This Diet?

As long as you are committed to following the Diverticulitis Diet, you will be able to feel relief from your condition within days following antibiotic treatments. You are encouraged to follow the first phase especially during the first few days of being diagnosed with diverticulitis. Following the first phase and as soon as your digestive tract is feeling better, you can start with the second phase by eating foods that are low in fiber. Eventually, your body particularly your digestive tract will recover. But consuming high fiber foods are then allowed to maintain a healthy digestive tract.

Other Dietary Considerations

While the Diverticulitis Diet is all about restricting yourself from consuming solid foods during the first few days after diagnosis following a low fiber diet, there are also other types of dietary considerations that you need to consider. Whether you are still following the liquid diet or the low carbohydrate diet, it is important that you keep yourself hydrated by drinking at least 8 glasses of water daily. Keeping yourself fully hydrated can help support healthy gastrointestinal health.

FAQs On Diverticulitis Diet

The Diverticulitis Diet is not something that you easily encounter daily as there are not too many people who suffer from this condition. Thus, we have collated common frequently asked questions about the Diverticulitis Diet.

#1 – Are there any risks when you follow the Diverticulitis Diet?
The Diverticulitis Diet can have some risks but not life-threatening at all. One of the risks is that you may feel a little weakness especially when you are still following the clear liquid diet stretched for a few days. The reason for this weakness is that you may not get enough nutrition inside your body due to consuming limited amounts of food. Aside from possible nutritional deficiency for a few days, the weakness may also be caused by low-calorie consumption during the clear liquid diet.

#2 – When can I go back to my normal diet?
There is no definite answer to this question. You can transition back to your normal diet as soon as you tolerate it. This means that there is a great deal of trial and error as well as observing your body's reactions to food before you can tell that you are indeed feeling better. For instance, after following the clear liquid diet and low carbohydrate diet for 5 days, you can try introducing normal foods into your body and observe your reactions.

If you feel bloated and nauseated after eating such foods, it means that you have not fully recovered yet. Continue with your low carbohydrate diet until you feel completely better.

#3 – Do I need to talk with a doctor?

If you are suffering from severe diverticulitis, then, yes, you need to talk to a doctor before you make any drastic changes in your diet. If you are still following the clear liquid diet, wait for your doctor's signal to add low fiber foods back into your diet so that your digestive tract can also adjust to the changes in your diet. Always seek help from a profession working with people who also have diverticulitis as the can offer you the best advice on what to do.

#4 – I have already re-introduced high fiber foods into my diet, but I am experiencing flareups again. What should I do?

The best thing that you need to do when you are having flare-ups is to see a doctor so that your doctor can make recommendations on what diet you need to do. If the flare-up is mild, you can revert to eating low fiber foods to reduce the symptoms. It is also crucial that you try to keep a food diary to keep track of the kinds of foods that you are eating. This will also help you find out which foods may have triggered your diverticulitis flare-up.

#5 – How do I add high fiber foods into my diet?

To avoid problems, avoid adding high fiber food immediately and drastically into your diet. Make sure that you do it in a staggered manner. When you introduce too much fiber all at once into your diet, it can cause gas and cramping that can make your situation even worse than before. Again, once you feel the discomfort following the reintroduction of high fiber foods, you need to revert to the two diet phases to cure your upset digestive tract.

Clear Liquid Recipes

1 – Healthier Apple Juice

Serves: 2
Preparation Time: 10 minutes

Ingredients:
- 8 medium apples, cored and quartered

Instructions:
1. Add the apples into a juicer and extract the juice according to the manufacturer's method.
2. Through a cheesecloth-lined strainer, strain the juice and transfer into 2 glasses.
3. Serve immediately.

Nutrition Information:
Calories per serving: 464; Carbohydrates: 123.6g; Protein: 2.4g; Fat: 1.6g; Sugar: 90g; Sodium: 123mg; Fiber: 21.6g

2 – Citrus Apple Juice

Serves: 2
Preparation Time: 10 minutes

Ingredients:
- 5 large apples, cored and chopped
- 1 small lemon
- 1 C. fresh orange juice

Instructions:
1. Place all the ingredients in a blender and pulse until well combined.
2. Through a cheesecloth-lined strainer, strain the juice and transfer into 2 glasses.
3. Serve immediately.

Nutrition Information:
Calories per serving: 348; Carbohydrates: 90.6g; Protein: 2.4g; Fat: 1.3g; Sugar: 68.6g; Sodium: 6mg; Fiber: 14g

3 – Richly Fruity Juice

Serves: 2
Preparation Time: 10 minutes

Ingredients:
- 5 large green apples, cored and sliced
- 2 C. seedless white grapes
- 2 tsp. fresh lime juice

Instructions:
1. Add all ingredients into a juicer and extract the juice according to the manufacturer's method.
2. Through a cheesecloth-lined strainer, strain the juice and transfer into 2 glasses.
3. Serve immediately.

Nutrition Information:
Calories per serving: 352; Carbohydrates: 92.8g; Protein: 2.1g; Fat: 1.3g; Sugar: 73g; Sodium: 7mg; Fiber: 14.3g

4 – Delish Grape Juice

Serves: 3
Preparation Time: 10 minutes

Ingredients:
- 2 C. white seedless grapes
- 1½ C. filtered water
- 6-8 ice cubes

Instructions:
1. Place all the ingredients in a blender and pulse until well combined.
2. Through a cheesecloth-lined strainer, strain the juice and transfer into 3 glasses.
3. Serve immediately.

Nutrition Information:
Calories per serving: 41; Carbohydrates: 10.5g; Protein: 0.4g; Fat: 0.2g; Sugar: 10g; Sodium: 1mg; Fiber: 10g

5 – Lemony Grape Juice

Serves: 3
Preparation Time: 10 minutes

Ingredients:
- 4 C. seedless white grapes
- 2 tbsp. fresh lemon juice

Instructions:
1. Place all the ingredients in a blender and pulse until well combined.
2. Through a cheesecloth-lined strainer, strain the juice and transfer into 3 glasses.
3. Serve immediately.

Nutrition Information:
Calories per serving: 85; Carbohydrates: 21.3g; Protein: 0.9g; Fat: 0.5g; Sugar: 20.1g; Sodium: 4mg; Fiber: 1.1g

6 – Holiday Special Juice

Serves: 4
Preparation Time: 10 minutes

Ingredients:
- 4 C. fresh cranberries
- 1 tbsp. fresh lemon juice
- 2 C. filtered water
- 1 tsp. raw honey

Instructions:
1. Place all the ingredients in a blender and pulse until well combined.
2. Through a cheesecloth-lined strainer, strain the juice and transfer into 4 glasses.
3. Serve immediately.

Nutrition Information:
Calories per serving: 66; Carbohydrates: 11.5g; Protein: 0g; Fat: 0g; Sugar: 5.5g; Sodium: 1mg; Fiber: 4g

7 – Vitamin C Rich Juice

Serves: 2
Preparation Time: 10 minutes

Ingredients:
- 8 oranges, peeled and sectioned

Instructions:
1. Add the orange sections into a juicer and extract the juice according to the manufacturer's method.
2. Through a cheesecloth-lined strainer, strain the juice and transfer into 2 glasses.
3. Serve immediately.

Nutrition Information:
Calories per serving: 346; Carbohydrates: 86.5g; Protein: 6.9g; Fat: 0.9g; Sugar: 68.8g; Sodium: 0mg; Fiber: 17.7g

8 – Incredible Fresh Juice

Serves: 4
Preparation Time: 10 minutes

Ingredients:
- 2 lb. carrots, trimmed and scrubbed
- 6 small oranges, peeled and sectioned

Instructions:
1. Add the carrots and orange sections into a juicer and extract the juice according to the manufacturer's method.
2. Through a cheesecloth-lined strainer, strain the juice and transfer into 4 glasses.
3. Serve immediately.

Nutrition Information:
Calories per serving: 183; Carbohydrates: 44.9g; Protein: 3.7g; Fat: 0.2g; Sugar: 29.1g; Sodium: 156mg; Fiber: 10.2g

9 – Favorite Summer Lemonade

Serves: 8
Preparation Time: 10 minutes

Ingredients:
- 8 C. filtered water
- ½ C. fresh lemon juice
- ¼ tsp. pure stevia extract
- Ice cubes, as required

Instructions:
1. In a pitcher, place the water, lemon juice and stevia and mix well.
2. Through a cheesecloth-lined strainer, strain the lemonade in another pitcher.
3. Refrigerate for 30-40 minutes.
4. Add ice cubes in serving glasses and fill with lemonade.
5. Serve chilled.

Nutrition Information:
Calories per serving: 4; Carbohydrates: 0.3g; Protein: 0.1g; Fat: 0.1g; Sugar: 0.3g; Sodium: 3mg; Fiber: 0.1g

10 – Ultimate Fruity Punch

Serves: 12
Preparation Time: 15 minutes

Ingredients:
- 3 C. fresh pineapple juice
- 2 C. fresh orange juice
- 1 C. fresh ruby red grapefruit juice
- ¼ C. fresh lime juice
- 2 C. seedless watermelon, cut into bite-sized chunks
- 2 C. fresh pineapple, cut into bite-sized chunks
- 2 oranges, peeled and cut into wedges
- 2 limes, quartered
- 1 lemon, sliced
- 2 (12-oz.) cans diet lemon lime soda
- Crushed ice, as required

Instructions:
1. In a large pitcher, add all ingredients except for soda cans and ice and stir to combine.
2. Set aside for 30 minutes.
3. Through a cheesecloth-lined strainer, strain the punch into another large pitcher.
4. Fill the glasses with ice and top with punch about ¾ of the way.
5. Add a splash of the soda and serve.

Nutrition Information:
Calories per serving: 95; Carbohydrates: 23.4g; Protein: 1.3g; Fat: 0.3g; Sugar: 18.3g; Sodium: 152mg; Fiber: 1.8g

11 – Thirst Quecher Sports Drink

Serves: 8
Preparation Time: 10 minutes

Ingredients:
- 7 C. spring water
- 1 C. fresh apple juice
- 2-3 tsp. fresh lime juice
- 2 tbsp. honey
- ¼ tsp. sea salt

Instructions:
1. In a large pitcher, add all ingredients and stir to combine.
2. Through a cheesecloth-lined strainer, strain the punch into another large pitcher.
3. Refrigerate to chill before serving.

Nutrition Information:
Calories per serving: 30; Carbohydrates: 7.8g; Protein: 0.1g; Fat: 0g; Sugar: 7.3g; Sodium: 60mg; Fiber: 0.1g

12 – Refreshing Sports Drink

Serves: 9
Preparation Time: 10 minutes

Ingredients:
- 8 C. fresh cold water, divided
- ¾ C. fresh orange juice
- ¼ C. fresh lemon juice
- ¼ C. fresh limes juice
- 3 tbsp. honey
- ½ tsp. salt

Instructions:
1. In a large pitcher, add all ingredients and stir to combine.
2. Through a cheesecloth-lined strainer, strain the punch into another large pitcher.
3. Refrigerate to chill before serving.

Nutrition Information:
Calories per serving: 33; Carbohydrates: 8.1g; Protein: 0.2g; Fat: 0.1g; Sugar: 7.6g; Sodium: 130mg; Fiber: 0.1g

13 – Perfect Sunny Day Tea

Serves: 6
Cooking Time: 3 minutes
Preparation Time: 15 minutes

Ingredients:
- 5 C. filtered water
- 5 green tea bags
- ¼ C. fresh lemon juice, strained
- ¼ C. fresh lime juice, strained
- ¼ C. honey
- Ice cubes, as required

Instructions:
1. In a medium pan, add 2 C. of water and bring to a boil.
2. Add in the tea bags and turn off the heat.
3. Immediately, cover the pan and steep for 3-4 minutes.
4. With a large spoon, gently press the tea bags against the pan to extract the tea completely.
5. Remove the tea bags from the pan and discard them.
6. Add honey and stir until dissolved.
7. In a large pitcher, place the tea, lemon and lime juice and stir to combine.
8. Add remaining cold water and stir to combine.
9. Refrigerate to chill before serving.
10. Add ice cubes in serving glasses and fill with tea.
11. Serve chilled.

Nutrition Information:
Calories per serving: 46; Carbohydrates: 12g; Protein: 0.1g; Fat: 0.1g; Sugar: 11.8g; Sodium: 3mg; Fiber: 0.1g

14 – Nutitious Green Tea

Serves: 4
Cooking Time: 4 minutes
Preparation Time: 15 minutes

Ingredients:
- 4 C. filtered water
- 4 orange peel strips
- 4 lemon peel strips
- 4 green tea bags
- 2 tsp. honey

Instructions:
1. In a medium pan, add the water, orange and lemon peel strips over medium-high heat and bring to a boil.
2. Reduce the heat to low and simmer, uncovered, for about 10 minutes.
3. With a slotted spoon, remove the orange and lemon peel strips and discard them.
4. Add in the tea bags and turn off the heat.
5. Immediately, cover the pan and steep for 3 minutes.
6. With a large spoon, gently press the tea bags against the pan to extract the tea completely.
7. Remove the tea bags from the pan and discard them.
8. Add honey and stir until dissolved.
9. Strain the tea in mugs and serve immediately.

Nutrition Information:
Calories per serving: 11; Carbohydrates: 3g; Protein: 0g; Fat: 0g; Sugar: 2.9g; Sodium: 0mg; Fiber: 0.1g

15 – Simple Black Tea

Serves: 2
Cooking Time: 3 minutes
Preparation Time: 10 minutes

Ingredients:
- 2 C. filtered water
- ½ tsp. black tea leaves
- 1 tsp. honey

Instructions:
1. In a pan, add the water and bring to a boil.
2. Stir in the tea leaves and turn off the heat.
3. Immediately, cover the pan and steep for 3 minutes.
4. Add honey and stir until dissolved.
5. Strain the tea in mugs and serve immediately.

Nutrition Information:
Calories per serving: 11; Carbohydrates: 2.9g; Protein: 0g; Fat: 0g; Sugar: 2.9g; Sodium: 123mg; Fiber: 0g

16 – Lemony Black Tea

Serves: 6
Preparation Time: 10 minutes

Ingredients:
- 1 tbsp. black tea leaves
- 1 lemon, sliced thinly
- 1 cinnamon stick
- 6 C. boiling water

Instructions:
1. In a large teapot, place the tea leaves, lemon slices and cinnamon stick.
2. Pour hot water over the ingredients and immediately cover the teapot.
3. Set aside for about 5 minutes to steep.
4. Strain the tea in mugs and serve immediately.

Nutrition Information:
Calories per serving: 1; Carbohydrates: 0.2g; Protein: 0g; Fat: 0g; Sugar: 0.1g; Sodium: 0mg; Fiber: 0.1g

17 – Metabolism Booster Coffee

Serves: 1
Cooking Time: 4 minutes
Preparation Time: 5 minutes

Ingredients:
- ¼ tsp. coffee powder
- 1¼ C. filtered water
- 1 tsp. fresh lemon juice
- 1 tsp. honey

Instructions:
1. In a small pan, add the water and coffee powder and bring it to boil.
2. Cook for about 1 minute.
3. Remove from the heat and pour into a serving mug.
4. Add the honey and lemon juice and stir until dissolved
5. Serve hot.

Nutrition Information:
Calories per serving: 23; Carbohydrates: 6g; Protein: 0.1g; Fat: 0g; Sugar: 5.9g; Sodium: 1mg; Fiber: 0g

18 – Best Homemade Broth

Serves: 8
Cooking Time: 2 hours 5 minutes
Preparation Time: 15 minutes

Ingredients:
- 1 (3-lb.) chicken, cut into pieces
- 5 medium carrots, peeled and cut into 2-inch pieces
- 4 celery stalks with leaves, cut into 2-inch pieces
- 6 fresh thyme sprigs
- 6 fresh parsley sprigs
- Salt, to taste
- 9 C. cold water

Instructions:
1. In a large pan, add all the ingredients over medium-high heat and bring to a boil.
2. Reduce the heat to medium-low and simmer, covered for about 2 hours, skimming the foam from the surface occasionally.
3. Through a fine-mesh sieve, strain the broth into a large bowl.
4. Serve hot.

Nutrition Information:
Calories per serving: 275; Carbohydrates: 4.3g; Protein: 49.7g; Fat: 5.2g; Sugar: 2g; Sodium: 160mg; Fiber: 1.2g

19 – Clean Testing Broth

Serves: 10
Cooking Time: 15 minutes
Preparation Time: 5 hours 50 minutes

Ingredients:
- 4 lb. chicken bones
- Salt, to taste
- 10 C. filtered water
- 2 tbsp. apple cider vinegar
- 1 lemon, quartered
- 3 bay leaves
- 3 tsp. ground turmeric
- 2 tbsp. peppercorns

Instructions:
1. Preheat the oven to 400 degrees F.
2. Arrange the bones onto a large baking sheet and sprinkle with salt.
3. Roast for about 45 minutes.
4. Remove from the oven and transfer the bones into a large pan.
5. Add the remaining ingredients and stir to combine.
6. Place the pan over medium-high heat and bring to a boil.
7. Reduce the heat to low and simmer, covered for about 4-5 hours, skimming the foam from the surface occasionally.
8. Through a fine-mesh sieve, strain the broth into a large bowl.
9. Serve hot.

Nutrition Information:
Calories per serving: 140; Carbohydrates: 0.6g; Protein: 25g; Fat: 2.6g; Sugar: 0.1g; Sodium: 73mg; Fiber: 0.1g

20 – Healing Broth

Serves: 12
Cooking Time: 15 minutes
Preparation Time: 10 hours 25 minutes

Ingredients:
- 3 tbsp. extra-virgin olive oil
- 2½ lb. chicken bones
- 4 celery stalks, chopped roughly
- 3 large carrots, peeled and chopped roughly
- 1 bay leaf
- 1 tbsp. black peppercorns
- 2 whole cloves
- 1 tbsp. apple cider vinegar
- Warm water, as required

Instructions:
1. In a Dutch oven, heat the oil over medium-high heat and sear the bones or about 3-5 minutes or until browned.
2. With a slotted spoon, transfer the bones into a bowl.
3. In the same pan, add the celery stalks and carrots and cook for about 15 minutes, stirring occasionally.
4. Add browned bones, bay leaf, black peppercorns, cloves and vinegar and stir to combine.
5. Add the enough warm water to cover the bones mixture completely and bring to a gentle boil.
6. Reduce the heat to low and simmer, covered for about 8-10 hours, skimming the foam from the surface occasionally.
7. Through a fine-mesh sieve, strain the broth into a large bowl.
8. Serve hot.

Nutrition Information:
Calories per serving: 67; Carbohydrates: 2g; Protein: 5.7g; Fat: 4.1g; Sugar: 1g; Sodium: 29mg; Fiber: 0.5g

21 – Veggie Lover's Broth

Serves: 10
Cooking Time: 15 minutes
Preparation Time: 2 hours 5 minutes

Ingredients:
- 4 carrots, peeled and chopped roughly
- 4 celery stalks, chopped roughly
- 3 parsnips, peeled and chopped roughly
- 2 large potatoes, peeled and chopped roughly
- 1 medium beet, trimmed and chopped roughly
- 1 large bunch fresh parsley
- 1 (1-inch) piece fresh ginger, sliced
- Filtered water, as required

Instructions:
1. In a large pan, add all the ingredients over medium-high heat.
2. Add enough water to cover the veggie mixture and bring to a boil.
3. Reduce the heat to low and simmer, covered for about 2-3 hours.
4. Through a fine-mesh sieve, strain the broth into a large bowl.
5. Serve hot.

Nutrition Information:
Calories per serving: 82; Carbohydrates: 19g; Protein: 1.9g; Fat: 0.2g; Sugar: 3.9g; Sodium: 37mg; Fiber: 3.7g

22 – Brain Healthy Broth

Serves: 6
Cooking Time: 10 minutes
Preparation Time: 12 hours 5 minutes

Ingredients:
- 12 C. filtered water
- 2 lb. non-oily fish heads and bones
- ¼ C. apple cider vinegar
- Sea salt, to taste

Instructions:
1. In a large pan, add all the ingredients over medium-high heat.
2. Add enough water to cover the veggie mixture and bring to a boil.
3. Reduce the heat to low and simmer, covered for about 10-12 hours, skimming the foam from the surface occasionally.
4. Through a fine-mesh sieve, strain the broth into a large bowl.
5. Serve hot.

Nutrition Information:
Calories per serving: 75; Carbohydrates: 0.1g; Protein: 13.4g; Fat: 1.7g; Sugar: 0g; Sodium: 253mg; Fiber: 0g

23 – Minerals Rich Broth

Serves: 8
Cooking Time: 2 hours 25 minutes
Preparation Time: 15 minutes

Ingredients:
- 5-7 lb. non-oily fish carcasses and heads
- 2 tbsp. olive oil
- 3 carrots, scrubbed and chopped roughly
- 2 celery stalks, chopped roughly
- 1 bay leaf
- 2 whole cloves
- 2 tsp. peppercorns
- 1 bunch fresh parsley
- 4 fresh thyme stems

Instructions:
1. In a large pan, heat the oil over medium-low heat and cook the carrots and celery for about 20 minutes, stirring occasionally.
2. Add the fish bones and enough water to cover by 1-inch and stir to combine.
3. Increase the heat to medium-high and bring to a boil.
4. Reduce the heat to low and simmer, covered for about 1-2 hours, skimming the foam from the surface occasionally.
5. Through a fine-mesh sieve, strain the broth into a large bowl.
6. Serve hot.

Nutrition Information:
Calories per serving: 113; Carbohydrates: 2.5g; Protein: 13.7g; Fat: 5.2g; Sugar: 1.2g; Sodium: 234mg; Fiber: 0.7g

24 – Holiday Favorite Gelatin

Serves: 6
Preparation Time: 15 minutes

Ingredients:
- 1 tbsp. grass-fed gelatin powder
- 1¾ C. fresh apple juice, warmed
- ¼ C. boiling water
- 1-2 drops fresh lemon juice

Instructions:
1. In a medium bowl, pour in the tbsp. of gelatin powder.
2. Add just enough warm apple juice to cover the gelatin and stir well.
3. Set aside for about 2-3 minutes or until it forms a thick syrup.
4. Add ¼ C. of the boiling water and stir until gelatin is dissolved completely.
5. Add the remaining juice and lemon juice and stir well.
6. Transfer the mixture into a parchment paper-lined baking dish and refrigerate for 2 hours or until the top is firm before serving.

Nutrition Information:
Calories per serving: 40; Carbohydrates: 8.2g; Protein: 1.9g; Fat: 0.1g; Sugar: 7g; Sodium: 5mg; Fiber: 0.2g

25 – Zesty Gelatin

Serves: 4
Cooking Time: 5 minutes
Preparation Time: 15 minutes

Ingredients:
- 1 tbsp. grass-fed gelatin powder
- ¾ C. filtered cold water, divided
- ¼ C. honey
- 1¼ C. fresh grapefruit juice
- Pinch of salt

Instructions:
1. In a bowl, soak the gelatin in ¼ C. of cold water. Set aside.
2. In a small pan, add the remaining ½ C. of water and honey over medium heat and bring to a boil.
3. Simmer for about 3 minutes or until honey is dissolved completely.
4. Remove from the heat and stir in the soaked gelatin until dissolved completely.
5. Set aside at room temperature to cool completely.
6. After cooling, stir in the grapefruit juice and salt.
7. Transfer the mixture into serving bowls and refrigerate for about 4 hours or until set.

Nutrition Information:
Calories per serving: 98; Carbohydrates: 23.3g; Protein: 3.3g; Fat: 0.1g; Sugar: 22.4g; Sodium: 43mg; Fiber: 0.8g

26 – 2-Ingredients Gelatin

Serves: 4
Preparation Time: 10 minutes

Ingredients:
- 1 tbsp. grass-fed tangerine gelatin powder
- 2¼ C. boiling water

Instructions:
1. In a large bowl, add the gelatin and boiling water and stir until dissolved completely.
2. Divide in serving bowls and refrigerate until set completely before serving.

Nutrition Information:
Calories per serving: 13; Carbohydrates: 0.4g; Protein: 2.8g; Fat: 0g; Sugar: 0.3g; Sodium: 3mg; Fiber: 0g

27 – Great Lemon Gelatin

Serves: 8
Preparation Time: 10 minutes

Ingredients:
- 3 tbsp. grass-fed gelatin powder
- 3 C. cold water, divided
- 1½ C. boiling water
- 1 C. plus 2 tbsp. fresh lemon juice
- 2 tsp. stevia extract

Instructions:
1. In a bowl, soak the gelatin in 1½ C. of cold water. Set aside for about 5 minutes.
2. Add boiling water and stir until gelatin is dissolved.
3. Add the remaining cold water, lemon juice and stevia extract and stir until dissolved completely.
4. Divide the mixture into 2 baking dishes and refrigerate until set before serving.

Nutrition Information:
Calories per serving: 24; Carbohydrates: 0.7g; Protein: 4.4g; Fat: 0.3g; Sugar: 0.7g; Sodium: 11mg; Fiber: 0.1g

28 – Weight Watcher's Gelatin

Serves: 8
Preparation Time: 10 minutes

Ingredients:
- 1 tbsp. grass-fed gelatin powder
- ¼ C. cold filtered water
- ¼ C. hot water
- 1 C. fresh grape juice

Instructions:
1. In a bowl, soak the gelatin in cold water. Set aside for about 5 minutes.
2. Add the hot water and mix well. Set aside for about 1-2 minutes.
3. Add the grape juice and mix well.
4. Divide in serving bowls and refrigerate until set completely before serving.

Nutrition Information:
Calories per serving: 17; Carbohydrates: 2.8g; Protein: 1.5g; Fat: 0g; Sugar: 2.7g; Sodium: 2mg; Fiber: 0g

29 – Beautifully Colored Gelatin

Serves: 10
Cooking Time: 5 minutes
Preparation Time: 10 minutes

Ingredients:
- 2 tbsp. grass-fed gelatin powder
- 4 C. fresh peach juice, divided
- 2 tbsp. honey

Instructions:
1. In a bowl, soak the gelatin in ½ C. of juice. Set aside for about 5 minutes.
2. In a medium pan, add the remaining juice over medium heat and bring to a gentle boil.
3. Remove from the heat and stir in honey.
4. Add the gelatin mixture and stir until dissolved.
5. Transfer the mixture into a large baking dish and refrigerate until set completely before serving.

Nutrition Information:
Calories per serving: 72; Carbohydrates: 16.1g; Protein: 2.2g; Fat: 0g; Sugar: 15.5g; Sodium: 9mg; Fiber: 0g

30 – Aromtic Cinnamon Gelatin

Serves: 2
Cooking Time: 5 minutes
Preparation Time: 10 minutes

Ingredients:
- 1 C. water
- 1 cinnamon stick
- 2 tsp. grass-fed gelatin powder
- 2 tbsp. honey

Instructions:
1. In a small pan, add the water over medium heat and bring to a boil.
2. Add in the cinnamon stick and turn off the heat.
3. Immediately, cover the pan and steep for 3 minutes.
4. Add the gelatin and beat until well combined.
5. Transfer the mixture into a baking dish and set aside to cool for about 2 hours.
6. Refrigerate to set before serving.

Nutrition Information:
Calories per serving: 76; Carbohydrates: 17.3g; Protein: 3.7g; Fat: 0g; Sugar: 17.3g; Sodium: 5mg; Fiber: 0g

Low-Residue Diet Recipes

31 – Bright Red Juice

Serves: 3
Preparation Time: 10 minutes

Ingredients:
- 6 tomatoes
- 2 carrots, peeled
- 1 celery stalk
- ¼ C. filtered water
- Pinch of salt and ground black pepper
- 2-3 ice cubes

Instructions:
1. Place all the ingredients in a blender and pulse until well combined.
2. Through a cheesecloth-lined strainer, strain the juice and transfer into 3 glasses.
3. Serve immediately.

Nutrition Information:
Calories per serving: 62; Carbohydrates: 13.7g; Protein: 2.5g; Fat: 0.5g; Sugar: 8.6g; Sodium: 95mg; Fiber: 4g

32 – Enticing Fresh Juice

Serves: 2
Preparation Time: 10 minutes

Ingredients:
- 3 C. fresh spinach
- 3 C. fresh arugula
- 1 large carrot, peeled and chopped roughly
- 2 celery stalks
- 1 lemon
- 1 (1-inch) piece fresh ginger

Instructions:
1. Add all ingredients into a juicer and extract the juice according to the manufacturer's method.
2. Through a cheesecloth-lined strainer, strain the juice and transfer into 2 glasses.
3. Serve immediately.

Nutrition Information:
Calories per serving: 36; Carbohydrates: 7.1g; Protein: 2.5g; Fat: 0.4g; Sugar: 2.8g; Sodium: 78mg; Fiber: 2.7g

33 – Super-Food Scramble

Serves: 3
Cooking Time: 7 minutes
Preparation Time: 10 minutes

Ingredients:
- 2 C. fresh spinach, chopped finely
- 1 tbsp. olive oil
- Salt and freshly ground black pepper, to taste
- ½ C. cooked salmon, chopped finely
- 4 eggs, beaten

Instructions:
1. In a skillet, heat the oil over high heat and cook the spinach with black pepper for about 2 minutes.
2. Stir in the salmon and reduce the heat to medium.
3. Add the eggs and cook for about 3-4 minutes, stirring frequently.
4. Serve immediately.

Nutrition Information:
Calories per serving: 179; Carbohydrates: 1.2g; Protein: 15.3g; Fat: 12.9g; Sugar: 0.5g; Sodium: 165mg; Fiber: 0.4g

34 – Family Favorite Scramble

Serves: 2
Cooking Time: 5 minutes
Preparation Time: 10 minutes

Ingredients:
- 4 eggs
- ¼ tsp. red pepper flakes, crushed
- Salt and freshly ground black pepper, to taste
- ¼ C. fresh basil, chopped
- ½ C. tomatoes, peeled, seeded and chopped
- 1 tbsp. olive oil

Instructions:
1. In a large bowl, add eggs, red pepper flakes, salt and black pepper and beat well.
2. Add the basil and tomatoes and stir to combine.
3. In a large non-stick skillet, heat the oil over medium-high heat.
4. Add the egg mixture and cook for about 3-5 minutes, stirring continuously.
5. Serve immediately.

Nutrition Information:
Calories per serving: 195; Carbohydrates: 2.6g; Protein: 11.6g; Fat: 15.9g; Sugar: 1.9g; Sodium: 203mg; Fiber: 0.7g

35 – Tasty Veggie Omelet

Serves: 4
Cooking Time: 25 minutes
Preparation Time: 15 minutes

Ingredients:
- 6 large eggs
- Sea salt and freshly ground black pepper, to taste
- ½ C. low-fat milk
- 1/3 C. fresh mushrooms, cut into slices
- 1/3 C. red bell pepper, seeded and chopped
- 1 tbsp. chives, minced

Instructions:
1. Preheat the oven to 350 degrees F. Lightly, grease a pie dish.
2. In a bowl, add the eggs, salt, black pepper and coconut oil and beat until well combined.
3. In another bowl, mix together the onion, bell pepper and mushrooms.
4. Transfer the egg mixture into the prepared pie dish evenly.
5. Top with vegetable mixture evenly and sprinkle with chives evenly.
6. Bake for about 20-25 minutes.
7. Remove from the oven and set aside for about 5 minutes.
8. With a knife, cut into equal sized wedges and serve.

Nutrition Information:
Calories per serving: 125; Carbohydrates: 3.1g; Protein: 10.8g; Fat: 7.8g; Sugar: 2.8g; Sodium: 158mg; Fiber: 0.2g

36 – Garden Veggies Quiche

Serves: 4
Cooking Time: 20 minutes
Preparation Time: 15 minutes

Ingredients:
- 6 eggs
- ½ C. low-fat milk
- Salt and freshly ground black pepper, to taste
- 2 C. fresh baby spinach, chopped
- ½ C. green bell pepper, seeded and chopped
- 1 scallion, chopped
- ¼ C. fresh parsley, chopped
- 1 tbsp. fresh chives, minced

Instructions:
1. Preheat the oven to 400 degrees F. Lightly grease a pie dish.
2. In a bowl, add eggs, almond milk, salt and black pepper and beat until well combined. Set aside.
3. In another bowl, add the vegetables and herbs and mix well.
4. In the bottom of prepared pie dish, place the veggie mixture evenly and top with the egg mixture.
5. Bake for about 20 minutes or until a wooden skewer inserted in the center comes out clean.
6. Remove pie dish from the oven and set aside for about 5 minutes before slicing.
7. Cut into desired sized wedges and serve warm.

Nutrition Information:
Calories per serving: 118; Carbohydrates: 4.3g; Protein: 10.1g; Fat: 7g; Sugar: 3g; Sodium: 160mg; Fiber: 0.8g

37 – Stunning Breakfast Frittata

Serves: 6
Cooking Time: 12 minutes
Preparation Time: 15 minutes

Ingredients:
- 8 eggs, beaten well
- 8 tbsp. low-fat milk
- Salt and freshly ground black pepper, to taste
- 2 oz. feta cheese, crumbled
- ½ C. low-fat mozzarella cheese, grated
- ¼ C. scallion, sliced
- 2 tsp. olive oil
- 1 large avocado, peeled, pitted and sliced lengthwise

Instructions:
1. Preheat the broiler of oven.
2. Arrange the oven rack about 4-5-inch from the heating element.
3. In a bowl, add the eggs, almond milk, salt and black pepper and beat until well combined.
4. In a heavy oven-proof frying skillet, heat the oil over medium-low heat.
5. Add the eggs and cook for about 2 minutes.
6. Add the mozzarella and scallion and cook for about 5 minutes.
7. Arrange the avocado slices over egg mixture and sprinkle with the feta cheese.
8. With ae lid, cover the skillet and cook about 3 minutes.
9. Remove lid and transfer the skillet into the oven.
10. Broil for about 2 minutes.
11. Remove from the oven and serve hot.

Nutrition Information:
Calories per serving: 207; Carbohydrates: 5.1g; Protein: 10.8g; Fat: 16.6g; Sugar: 2.2g; Sodium: 241mg; Fiber: 2.4g

38 – Fluffy Pumpkin Pancakes

Serves: 10
Cooking Time: 40 minutes
Preparation Time: 10 minutes

Ingredients:
- 2 eggs
- 1 C. buckwheat flour
- 1 tbsp. baking powder
- 1 tsp. pumpkin pie spice
- ½ tsp. salt
- 1 C. pumpkin puree
- ¾ C. plus 2 tbsp. low-fat milk
- 3 tbsp. pure maple syrup
- 2 tbsp. olive oil
- 1 tsp. vanilla extract

Instructions:
1. In a blender, add all ingredients and pulse until well combined.
2. Transfer the mixture into a bowl and set aside for about 10 minutes.
3. Heat a greased non-stick skillet over medium heat.
4. Place about ¼ C. of the mixture and spread in an even circle.
5. Cook for about 2 minutes per side.
6. Repeat with the remaining mixture.
7. Serve warm.

Nutrition Information:
Calories per serving: 113; Carbohydrates: 16.5g; Protein: 3.6g; Fat: 4.4g; Sugar: 5.9g; Sodium: 143mg; Fiber: 2g

39 – Sper-Tasty Chicken Muffins

Serves: 8
Cooking Time: 45 minutes
Preparation Time: 15 minutes

Ingredients:
- 8 eggs
- Salt and freshly ground black pepper, as required
- 2 tbsp. filtered water
- 7 oz. cooked chicken, chopped finely
- 1½ C. fresh spinach, chopped
- 1 C. green bell pepper, seeded and chopped finely
- 2 tbsp. fresh parsley, chopped finely

Instructions:
1. Preheat the oven to 350 degrees F. Grease 8 C. of a muffin tin.
2. In a bowl, add eggs, salt, black pepper and water and beat until well combined.
3. Add the chicken, spinach, bell pepper and parsley and stir to combine.
4. Transfer the mixture into the prepared muffin C. evenly.
5. Bake for about 18-20 minutes or until golden brown.
6. Remove the muffin tin from oven and place onto a wire rack to cool for about 10 minutes.
7. Carefully invert the muffins onto a platter and serve warm.

Nutrition Information:
Calories per serving: 107; Carbohydrates: 1.7g; Protein: 13.1g; Fat: 5.2g; Sugar: 1.1g; Sodium: 102mg; Fiber: 0.4g

40 – Classic Zucchini Bread

Serves: 24
Cooking Time: 15 minutes
Preparation Time: 45 minutes

Ingredients:
- 3 C. all-purpose flour
- 2 tsp. baking soda
- 1 tsp. ground cinnamon
- 1 tsp. ground nutmeg
- 2 C. Splenda
- 1 C. olive oil
- 3 eggs, beaten
- 2 tsp. vanilla extract
- 2 C. zucchini, peeled, seeded and grated

Instructions:
1. Preheat the oven to 325 degrees F. Arrange a rack in the center of oven. Grease 2 loaf pans.
2. In a medium bowl, mix together the flour, baking soda and spices.
3. In another large bowl, add the Splenda and oil and beat until well combined.
4. Add the eggs and vanilla extract and beat until well combined.
5. Add the flour mixture and mix until just combined.
6. Gently, fold in the zucchini.
7. Place the mixture into the bread loaf pans evenly.
8. Bake for about 45-50 minutes or until a toothpick inserted in the center of bread comes out clean.
9. Remove the bread pans from oven and place onto a wire rack to cool for about 15 minutes.
10. Carefully, invert the breads onto the wire rack to cool completely before slicing.
11. With a sharp knife, cut each bread loaf into desired-sized slices and serve.

Nutrition Information:
Calories per serving: 219; Carbohydrates: 28.4g; Protein: 16.3g; Fat: 9.2g; Sugar: 16.3g; Sodium: 113mg; Fiber: 0.6g

41 – Greek Inspired Cucumber Salad

Serves: 4
Preparation Time: 10 minutes

Ingredients:
- 4 medium cucumbers, peeled, seeded and chopped
- ½ C. low-fat Greek yogurt
- 1½ tbsp. fresh dill, chopped
- 1 tbsp. fresh lemon juice
- Salt and freshly ground black pepper, as required

Instructions:
1. In a large bowl, add all the ingredients and mix well.
2. Serve immediately.

Nutrition Information:
Calories per serving: 71; Carbohydrates: 13.8g; Protein:4g; Fat: 0.8g; Sugar: 7.3g; Sodium: 69mg; Fiber: 1.7g

42 – Light Veggie Salad

Serves: 5
Preparation Time: 10 minutes

Ingredients:

- 2 C. cucumbers, peeled, seeded and chopped
- 2 C. red tomatoes, peeled, seeded and chopped
- 2 tbsp. extra-virgin olive oil
- 2 tbsp. fresh lime juice
- Salt, to taste

Instructions:

1. In a large serving bowl, add all the ingredients and toss to coat well.
2. Serve immediately.

Nutrition Information:

Calories per serving: 68; Carbohydrates: 04.4g; Protein: 0.9g; Fat: 5.8g; Sugar: 2.6g; Sodium: 35mg; Fiber: 1.1g

43 – Eastern European Soup

Serves: 3
Cooking Time: 5 minutes
Preparation Time: 10 minutes

Ingredients:
- 2 C. fat-free yogurt
- 4 tsp. fresh lemon juice
- 2 C. beets, trimmed, peeled and chopped
- 2 tbsp. fresh dill
- Salt, as required
- 1 tbsp. fresh chives, minced

Instructions:
1. In a high-speed blender, add all ingredients except for chives and pulse until smooth.
2. Transfer the soup into a pan over medium heat and cook for about 3-5 minutes or until heated through.
3. Serve immediately with the garnishing of chives.

Nutrition Information:
Calories per serving: 149; Carbohydrates: 25.2g; Protein: 11.8g; Fat: 0.6g; Sugar: 21.7g; Sodium: 269mg; Fiber: 2.5g

44 – Citrus Glazed Carrots

Serves: 6
Cooking Time: 15 minutes
Preparation Time: 15 minutes

Ingredients:
- 1½ lb. carrots, peeled and sliced into ½-inch pieces diagonally
- ½ C. water
- 2 tbsp. olive oil
- Salt, to taste
- 3 tbsp. fresh orange juice

Instructions:
1. In a large skillet, add the carrots, water, boil and salt over medium heat and bring to a boil.
2. Reduce heat to low and simmer; covered for about 6 minutes.
3. Add the orange juice and stir to combine.
4. Increase the heat to high and cook, uncovered for about 5-8 minutes, tossing frequently.
5. Serve immediately.

Nutrition Information:
Calories per serving: 90; Carbohydrates: 12g; Protein: 1g; Fat: 4.7g; Sugar: 6.2g; Sodium: 106mg; Fiber: 2.8g

45 – Braised Asparagus

Serves: 2
Cooking Time: 8 minutes
Preparation Time: 10 minutes

Ingredients:
- ½ C. chicken bone broth
- 1 tbsp. olive oil
- 1 (½-inch) lemon peel
- 1 C. asparagus, trimmed

Instructions:
1. In a small pan add the broth, oil and lemon peel over medium heat and bring to a boil.
2. Add the asparagus and cook, covered for about 3-4 minutes.
3. Discard the lemon peel and serve.

Nutrition Information:
Calories per serving: 82; Carbohydrates: 2.6g; Protein: 3.7g; Fat: 7.1g; Sugar: 1.3g; Sodium: 25mg; Fiber: 1.4g

46 – Spring Flavored Pasta

Serves: 4
Cooking Time: 10 minutes
Preparation Time: 10 minutes

Ingredients:
- 2 tbsp. olive oil
- 1 lb. asparagus, trimmed and cut into 1½-inch pieces
- Salt and freshly ground black pepper, to taste
- ½ lb. cooked hot pasta, drained

Instructions:
1. In a large cast-iron skillet, heat the oil over medium heat and cook the asparagus, salt and black pepper for about 8-10 minutes, stirring occasionally.
2. Place the hot pasta and toss to coat well.
3. Serve immediately.

Nutrition Information:
Calories per serving: 246 Carbohydrates: 35.2g; Protein: 8.9g; Fat: 8.4g; Sugar: 2.1g; Sodium: 17mg; Fiber: 2.4g

47 – Versatile Mac 'n Cheese

Serves: 0
Cooking Time: 12 minutes
Preparation Time: 15 minutes

Ingredients:
- 2 C. elbow macaroni
- 1½ s butternut squash, peeled and cubed
- 1 C. low-fat Swiss cheese, shredded
- 1/3 C. low-fat milk
- 1 tbsp. olive oil
- Salt and freshly ground black pepper, to taste

Instructions:
1. In a large pan of the salted boiling water, cook the macaroni for about 8-10 minutes.
2. Drain the macaroni and transfer into a bowl.
3. Meanwhile, in a pan of the boiling water, cook the squash cubes for about 6 minutes or until soft.
4. Drain the squash cubes completely and return to the same pan.
5. With a masher, mash the squash and place over low heat.
6. Add the cheese and milk and cook for about 2-3 minutes, stirring continuously.
7. Add the macaroni, oil, salt and black pepper and stir to combine.
8. Remove from the heat and serve hot.

Nutrition Information:
Calories per serving: 321; Carbohydrates: 40g; Protein: 14g; Fat: 11.9g; Sugar: 3.7g; Sodium: 65mg; Fiber: 2.4g

48 – Gluten-Free Curry

Serves: 6
Cooking Time: 20 minutes
Preparation Time: 15 minutes

Ingredients:
- 2 C. tomatoes, peeled, seeded and chopped
- 1½ C. water
- 2 tbsp. olive oil
- 1 tsp. fresh ginger, chopped
- ¼ tsp. ground turmeric
- 2 C. fresh shiitake mushrooms, sliced
- 5 C. fresh button mushrooms, sliced
- ¼ C. fat-free yogurt, whipped
- Salt and freshly ground black pepper, to taste

Instructions:
1. In a food processor, add the tomatoes and ¼ C. of water and pulse until a smooth paste forms.
2. In a pan, heat the oil over medium heat and sauté the ginger and turmeric for about 1 minute.
3. Add the tomato paste and cook for about 5 minutes.
4. Stir in the mushrooms, yogurt and remaining water and bring to a boil.
5. Cook for about 10-12 minutes, stirring occasionally.
6. Season with the salt and black pepper and remove from the heat.
7. Serve hot.

Nutrition Information:
Calories per serving: 70; Carbohydrates: 5.3g; Protein: 3g; Fat: 5g; Sugar: 3.4g; Sodium: 41mg; Fiber: 1.4g

49 – New Year's Luncheon Meal

Serves: 2
Preparation Time: 10 minutes

Ingredients:
- 1 large avocado, halved and pitted
- 1 (5-oz.) can water-packed tuna, drained and flaked
- 3 tbsp. fat-free yogurt
- 2 tbsp. fresh lemon juice
- 1 tsp. fresh parsley, chopped finely
- Salt and freshly ground black pepper, to taste

Instructions:
1. Carefully, remove abut about 2-3 tbsp. of flesh from each avocado half.
2. Arrange the avocado halves onto a platter and drizzle each with 1 tsp. of lemon juice.
3. Chop the avocado flesh and transfer into a bowl.
4. In the bowl of avocado flesh, add tuna, yogurt, parsley, remaining lemon juice, salt, and black pepper, and stir to combine.
5. Divide the tuna mixture in both avocado halves evenly.
6. Serve immediately.

Nutrition Information:
Calories per serving: 215; Carbohydrates: 7g; Protein: 20.6g; Fat: 11.8g; Sugar: 2.4g; Sodium: 137mg; Fiber: 3.2g

50 – Entertaining Wraps

Serves: 5
Cooking Time: 10 minutes
Preparation Time: 15 minutes

Ingredients:
For Chicken:
- 2 tbsp. olive oil
- 1 tsp. fresh ginger, minced
- 1¼ lb. ground chicken
- Salt and freshly ground black pepper, to taste

For Wraps:
- 10 romaine lettuce leaves
- 1½ C. carrot, peeled and julienned
- 2 tbsp. fresh parsley, chopped finely
- 2 tbsp. fresh lime juice

Instructions:
1. In a skillet, heat the oil over medium heat and sauté the ginger for about 1 minute.
2. Add the ground chicken, salt, and black pepper and cook for about 7-9 minutes, breaking up the meat into smaller pieces with a wooden spoon.
3. Remove from the heat and set aside to cool.
4. Arrange the lettuce leaves onto serving plates.
5. Place the cooked chicken over each lettuce leaf and top with carrot and cilantro.
6. Drizzle with lime juice and serve immediately.

Nutrition Information:
Calories per serving: 280; Carbohydrates: 3.8g; Protein: 33.2g; Fat: 14g; Sugar: 1.7g; Sodium: 153mg; Fiber: 0.9g

51 – Outdoor Chicken Kabobs

Serves: 4
Cooking Time: 7 minutes
Preparation Time: 15 minutes

Ingredients:
- ¼ C. low-fat Parmesan cheese, grated
- 3 tbsp. olive oil
- 1 C. fresh basil leaves, chopped
- Salt and freshly ground black pepper, to taste
- 1¼ lb. boneless, skinless chicken breast, cut into 1-inch cubes

Instructions:
1. In a food processor, add the cheese, oil, garlic, basil, salt, and black pepper, and pulse until smooth.
2. Transfer the basil mixture into a large bowl.
3. Add the chicken cubes and mix well.
4. Cover the bowl and refrigerate to marinate for at least 4-5 hours.
5. Preheat the grill to medium-high heat. Generously, grease the grill grate.
6. Thread the chicken cubes onto pre-soaked wooden skewers.
7. Place the skewers onto the grill and cook for about 3-4 minutes.
8. Flip and cook for about 2-3 minutes more.
9. Remove from the grill and place onto a platter for about 5 minutes before serving.
10. Serve hot.

Nutrition Information:
Calories per serving: 270; Carbohydrates: 0.3g; Protein: 31.5g; Fat: 15.3g; Sugar: 0g; Sodium: 207mg; Fiber: 0.1g

52 – Flavorful Shrimp Kabobs

Serves: 4
Cooking Time: 8 minutes
Preparation Time: 15 minutes

Ingredients:
- ¼ C. olive oil
- 2 tbsp. fresh lime juice
- 1 tsp. honey
- ½ tsp. paprika
- ¼ tsp. ground cumin
- Salt and freshly ground black pepper, to taste
- 1 lb. medium raw shrimp, peeled and deveined

Instructions:
1. In a large bowl, add all the ingredients except for shrimp and mix well.
2. Add the shrimp and coat with the herb mixture generously.
3. Refrigerate to marinate for at least 30 minutes.
4. Preheat the grill to medium-high heat. Grease the grill grate.
5. Thread the shrimp onto pre-soaked wooden skewers.
6. Place the skewers onto the grill and cook for about 2-4 minutes per side.
7. Remove from the grill and place onto a platter for about 5 minutes before serving.

Nutrition Information:
Calories per serving: 250; Carbohydrates: 3.4g; Protein: 25.9g; Fat: 14.6g; Sugar: 01.5g; Sodium: 316mg; Fiber: 0.1g

53 – Pan-Seared Scallops

Serves: 4
Cooking Time: 7 minutes
Preparation Time: 15 minutes

Ingredients:
- 1¼ lb. fresh sea scallops, side muscles removed
- Salt and freshly ground black pepper, to taste
- 2 tbsp. olive oil
- 1 tbsp. fresh parsley, minced

Instructions:
1. Sprinkle the scallops with salt and black pepper.
2. In a large skillet, heat the oil over medium-high heat and cook the scallops for about 2-3 minutes per side.
3. Stir in the parsley and remove from the heat.
4. Serve hot.

Nutrition Information:
Calories per serving: 185; Carbohydrates: 3.4g; Protein: 23.8g; Fat: 8.1g; Sugar: 0g; Sodium: 268mg; Fiber: 0g

54 – Mediteranean Shrimp Salad

Serves: 5
Cooking Time: 3 minutes
Preparation Time: 15 minutes

Ingredients:
- 1 lb. shrimp, peeled and deveined
- 1 lemon, quartered
- 2 tbsp. olive oil
- 2 tsp. fresh lemon juice
- Salt and freshly ground black pepper, to taste
- 3 tomatoes, peeled, seeded and sliced
- ¼ C. olives, pitted
- ¼ C. fresh cilantro, chopped finely

Instructions:
1. In a pan of the lightly salted water, add the quartered lemon and bring to a boil.
2. Add the shrimp and cook for about 2-3 minutes or until pink and opaque.
3. With a slotted spoon, transfer the shrimp into a bowl of ice water to stop the cooking process.
4. Drain the shrimp completely and then pat dry with paper towels.
5. In a small bowl, add the oil, lemon juice, salt, and black pepper, and beat until well combined.
6. Divide the shrimp, tomato, olives, and cilantro onto serving plates.
7. Drizzle with oil mixture and serve.

Nutrition Information:
Calories per serving: 178; Carbohydrates: 5g; Protein: 21.4g; Fat: 8g; Sugar: 2.1g; Sodium: 315mg; Fiber: 1.2g

55 – Helth Conscious People's Salad

Serves: 2
Preparation Time: 15 minutes

Ingredients:
- ¼ C. low-fat mozzarella cheese, cubed
- ¼ C. tomato, peeled, seeded and chopped
- 1 tbsp. fresh dill, chopped
- 1 tsp. fresh lemon juice
- Salt, to taste
- 6 oz. cooked salmon, chopped

Instructions:
1. In a small bowl, add all the ingredients and stir to combine.
2. Serve immediately.

Nutrition Information:
Calories per serving: 131; Carbohydrates: 1.9g; Protein: 18g; Fat: 6g; Sugar: 0.6g; Sodium: 141mg; Fiber: 0.5g

56 – Italian Pasta Soup

Serves: 5
Cooking Time: 25 minutes
Preparation Time: 15 minutes

Ingredients:
- 1 potato, peeled and chopped
- 1 carrot, peeled and chopped
- 5¼ C. chicken bone broth
- ½ C. tomato, peeled, seeded and chopped
- ¾ lb. asparagus tips
- ½ C. cooked small pasta
- Salt and freshly ground black pepper, to taste

Instructions:
1. In a pan, add the potato, carrot and broth over medium-high heat and bring to a boil.
2. Reduce the heat to low and cook, covered for about 15 minutes or until vegetables become tender.
3. Add the tomatoes and asparagus and cook or about 4-5 minutes.
4. Stir in the cooked pasta, salt and black pepper and cook for about 2-3 minutes.
5. Serve hot.

Nutrition Information:
Calories per serving: 147; Carbohydrates: 23.2g; Protein: 13.6g; Fat: 0.5g; Sugar: 3.5g; Sodium: 108mg; Fiber: 3g

57 – Pure Comfort Soup

Serves: 4
Cooking Time: 20 minutes
Preparation Time: 10 minutes

Ingredients:
- 6 C. chicken bone broth
- 1/3 C. orzo
- 6 large egg yolks
- 1½ C. cooked chicken, shredded
- ¼ C. fresh lemon juice
- Salt and freshly ground black pepper, to taste

Instructions:
1. In a large pan, add the broth over medium-high heat and bring to a boil.
2. Add the pasta and cook for about 8-9 minutes.
3. In a slowly, add in 1 C. of the hot broth, beating continuously.
4. Add the egg mixture to the pan, stirring continuously.
5. Reduce the heat to medium and cook for about 5-7 minutes, stirring, frequently.
6. Stir in the cooked chicken, salt and black pepper and cook for about 1-2 minutes.
7. Remove from the heat and serve hot.

Nutrition Information:
Calories per serving: 269; Carbohydrates: 11.9g; Protein: 34.6g; Fat: 8.7g; Sugar: 1.2g; Sodium: 230mg; Fiber: 0.6g

58 – Goof-for-You Stew

Serves: 8
Cooking Time: 18 minutes
Preparation Time: 15 minutes

Ingredients:
- 2½ C. fresh tomatoes, peeled, seeded and chopped
- 4 C. fish bone broth
- 1 lb. salmon fillets, cubed
- 1 lb. shrimp, peeled and deveined
- 2 tbsp. fresh lime juice
- Salt and freshly ground black pepper, to taste
- 3 tbsp. fresh parsley, chopped

Instructions:
1. In a large soup pan, add the tomatoes and broth and bring to a boil.
2. Reduce the heat to medium and simmer for about 5 minutes.
3. Add the salmon and simmer for about 3-4 minutes.
4. Stir in the shrimp and cook for about 4-5 minutes.
5. Stir in lemon juice, salt, and black pepper, and remove from heat.
6. Serve hot with the garnishing of parsley.

Nutrition Information:
Calories per serving: 173; Carbohydrates: 3.2g; Protein: 27.1g; Fat: 5.5g; Sugar: 1.5g; Sodium: 368mg; Fiber: 0.7g

59 – Zero-Fiber Chicken Dish

Serves: 6
Cooking Time: 10 minutes
Preparation Time: 16 minutes

Ingredients:
- 4 (6-oz.) boneless, skinless chicken breast halves
- Salt and freshly ground black pepper, to taste
- 2 tbsp. olive oil

Instructions:
1. Season each chicken breast half with salt and black pepper evenly.
2. Place chicken breast halves over a rack set in a rimmed baking sheet.
3. Refrigerate for at least 30 minutes.
4. Remove from refrigerator and pat dry with paper towels.
5. In a skillet, heat the oil over medium-low heat.
6. Place the chicken breast halves, smooth-side down, and cook for about 9-10 minutes, without moving.
7. Flip the chicken breasts and cook for about 6 minutes or until cooked through.
8. Remove from the heat and let the chicken stand in the pan for about 3 minutes.
9. Now, place the chicken breasts onto a cutting board.
10. Cut each chicken breast into slices and serve.

Nutrition Information:
Calories per serving: 255; Carbohydrates: 0g; Protein: 32.8g; Fat: 13.1g; Sugar: 0g; Sodium: 125mg; Fiber: 0g

60 – Amazing Chicken Platter

Serves: 6
Cooking Time: 18 minutes
Preparation Time: 15 minutes

Ingredients:
- 2 tbsp. olive oil, divided
- 4 (4-oz.) boneless, skinless chicken breasts, cut into small pieces
- Salt and freshly ground black pepper, to taste
- 1 tsp. fresh ginger, grated
- 4 C. fresh mushrooms, sliced
- 1 C. chicken bone broth

Instructions:
1. In a large skillet, heat 1 tbsp. of oil over medium-high heat and stir fry the chicken pieces, salt, and black pepper for about 4-5 minutes or until golden-brown.
2. With a slotted spoon, transfer the chicken pieces onto a plate.
3. In the same skillet, heat the remaining oil over medium heat and sauté the onion, ginger for about 1 minute.
4. Add the mushrooms and cook for about 6-7 minutes, stirring frequently.
5. Add the cooked chicken and coconut milk and stir fry for about 3-4 minutes
6. Add in the salt and black pepper and remove from the heat.
7. Serve hot.

Nutrition Information:
Calories per serving: 200; Carbohydrates: 1.6g; Protein: 24.8g; Fat: 10.4g; Sugar: 0.8g; Sodium: 111mg; Fiber: 0.5g

61 – Colorful Chicken Dinner

Serves: 6
Cooking Time: 20 minutes
Preparation Time: 15 minutes

Ingredients:
- 3 tbsp. olive oil, divided
- 1 large yellow bell pepper, seeded and sliced
- 1 large red bell pepper, seeded and sliced
- 1 large green bell pepper, seeded and sliced
- 1 lb. boneless, skinless chicken breasts, sliced thinly
- 1 tsp. dried oregano, crushed
- ¼ tsp. garlic powder
- ¼ tsp. ground cumin
- Salt and freshly ground black pepper, to taste
- ¼ C. chicken bone broth

Instructions:
1. In a skillet, heat 1 tbsp. of oil over medium-high heat and cook the bell peppers for about 4-5 minutes.
2. With a slotted spoon, transfer the peppers mixture onto a plate.
3. In the same skillet, heat the remaining over medium-high heat and cook the chicken for about 8 minutes, stirring frequently.
4. Stir in the thyme, spices, salt, black pepper, and broth, and bring to a boil.
5. Add the peppers mixture and stir to combine.
6. Reduce the heat to medium and cook for about 3-5 minutes or until all the liquid is absorbed, stirring occasionally.
7. Serve immediately.

Nutrition Information:
Calories per serving: 226; Carbohydrates: 4.8g; Protein: 22.9g; Fat: 12.8g; Sugar: 3g; Sodium: 98mg; Fiber: 0.9g

62 – Easiest Tuna Salad

Serves: 4
Preparation Time: 15 minutes

Ingredients:
For Dressing:
- 2 tbsp. fresh dill, minced
- 2 tbsp. olive oil
- 1 tbsp. fresh lime juice
- Salt and freshly ground black pepper, to taste

For Salad:
- 2 (6-oz.) cans water-packed tuna, drained and flaked
- 6 hard-boiled eggs, peeled and sliced
- 1 C. tomato, peeled, seeded and chopped
- 1 large cucumber, peeled, seeded and sliced

Instructions:
1. For dressing: in a small bowl, add all the ingredients and beat until well combined.
2. For salad: in another large serving bowl, add all the ingredients and mix well.
3. Divide the tuna mixture onto serving plates.
4. Drizzle with dressing and serve.

Nutrition Information:
Calories per serving: 277; Carbohydrates: 5.9g; Protein: 31.2g; Fat: 14.5g; Sugar: 3g; Sodium: 181mg; Fiber: 1.1g

63 – Lemony Salmon

Serves: 4
Cooking Time: 14 minutes
Preparation Time: 10 minutes

Ingredients:
- 1 tbsp. fresh lemon zest, grated
- 2 tbsp. extra-virgin olive oil
- 2 tbsp. fresh lemon juice
- Salt and freshly ground black pepper, to taste
- 4 (6-oz.) boneless, skinless salmon fillets

Instructions:
1. Preheat the grill to medium-high heat. Grease the grill grate.
2. In a bowl, place all ingredients except for salmon fillets and mix well.
3. Add the salmon fillets and coat with garlic mixture generously.
4. Place the salmon fillets onto grill and cook for about 6-7 minutes per side.
5. Serve hot.

Nutrition Information:
Calories per serving: 290; Carbohydrates: 1g; Protein: 33.2g; Fat: 21.5g; Sugar: 0.3g; Sodium: 116mg; Fiber: 0.2g

64 – Herbed Salmon

Serves: 4
Cooking Time: 8 minutes
Preparation Time: 10 minutes

Ingredients:
- 1 tsp. dried oregano, crushed
- 1 tsp. dried basil, crushed
- Salt and freshly ground black pepper, to taste
- ¼ C. olive oil
- 2 tbsp. fresh lemon juice
- 4 (4-oz.) salmon fillets

Instructions:
1. In a large bowl, add all ingredients except for salmon and mix well.
2. Add the salmon and coat with marinade generously.
3. Cover the bowl and refrigerate to marinate for at least 1 hour.
4. Preheat the grill to medium-high heat. Grease the grill grate.
5. Place the salmon onto the grill and cook for about 4 minutes per side.
6. Serve hot.

Nutrition Information:
Calories per serving: 261; Carbohydrates: 0.4g; Protein: 22.1g; Fat: 19.7g; Sugar: 0.2g; Sodium: 80mg; Fiber: 0.2g

65 – Delicious Combo Dinner

Serves: 5
Cooking Time: 15 minutes
Preparation Time: 15 minutes

Ingredients:
- 2 tbsp. olive oil
- 1 lb. prawns, peeled and deveined
- 1 lb. asparagus, trimmed
- Salt and freshly ground black pepper, to taste
- 1 tsp. fresh ginger, minced
- 2 tbsp. fresh lemon juice

Instructions:
1. In a skillet, heat 1 tbsp. of oil over medium-high heat and cook the prawns with salt and black pepper for about 3-4 minutes.
2. With a slotted spoon, transfer the prawns into a bowl. Set aside.
3. In the same skillet, heat the remaining oil over medium-high heat and cook the asparagus, ginger, salt and black pepper for about 6-8 minutes, stirring frequently.
4. Stir in the prawns and cook for about 1 minute.
5. Stir in the lemon juice and remove from the heat.
6. Serve hot.

Nutrition Information:
Calories per serving: 176; Carbohydrates: 5.1g; Protein: 22.7g; Fat: 7.3g; Sugar: 1.9g; Sodium: 255mg; Fiber: 1.9g

High-Fiber Recipes

66 – Vitamins Packed Green Juice

Serves: 2
Preparation Time: 10 minutes

Ingredients:
- 6 pears, cored and chopped
- 3 celery stalks
- 3 C. fresh kale
- 2 tbsp. fresh parsley

Instructions:
1. Place all the ingredients in a blender and pulse until well combined.
2. Through a cheesecloth-lined strainer, strain the juice and transfer into 2 glasses.
3. Serve immediately.

Nutrition Information:
Calories per serving: 209; Carbohydrates: 50.5g; Protein: 5.1g; Fat: 0.9g; Sugar: 26.2g; Sodium: 66mg; Fiber: 15.2g

67 – Healthier Breakfast Juice

Serves: 2
Preparation Time: 10 minutes

Ingredients:
- 2 large Granny Smith apples, cored and sliced
- 4 medium carrots, peeled and chopped
- 2 medium grapefruit, peeled and seeded
- 1 C. fresh kale
- 1 tsp. fresh lemon juice

Instructions:
1. Place all the ingredients in a blender and pulse until well combined.
2. Through a cheesecloth-lined strainer, strain the juice and transfer into 2 glasses.
3. Serve immediately.

Nutrition Information:
Calories per serving: 265; Carbohydrates: 67g; Protein: 4.2g; Fat: o.7g; Sugar: 47.1g; Sodium: 101mg; Fiber: 11.7g

68 – Summer Perfect Smoothie

Serves: 2
Preparation Time: 10 minutes

Ingredients:
- 2 C. frozen peaches, pitted
- ½ C. rolled oats
- ¼ tsp. ground cinnamon
- 1½ C. plain yogurt
- ½ C. fresh orange Juice

Instructions:
1. In a high-speed blender, add all the ingredients and pulse until smooth and creamy.
2. Transfer the smoothie into 2 serving glasses and serve immediately.

Nutrition Information:
Calories per serving: 328; Carbohydrates: 56g; Protein: 15g; Fat: 4.1g; Sugar: 41g; Sodium: 131mg; Fiber: 5g

69 – Filling Breakfast Smoothie

Serves: 4
Preparation Time: 10 minutes

Ingredients:
- 2 oz. rolled oats
- 4 apples, peeled, cored and chopped roughly
- 4 scoops unsweetened vegan protein powder
- 1 tsp. stevia powder
- 1 tsp. ground cinnamon
- 1 tsp. ground nutmeg
- 17 oz. plain yogurt
- 2 C. milk

Instructions:
1. In a high-speed blender, add all the ingredients and pulse until smooth and creamy.
2. Transfer the smoothie into 4 serving glasses and serve immediately.

Nutrition Information:
Calories per serving: 437; Carbohydrates: 55.6g; Protein: 38.7g; Fat: 6.6g; Sugar: 37.5g; Sodium: 409mg; Fiber: 7.3g

70 – Bright Green Breakfast Bowl

Serves: 2
Preparation Time: 10 minutes

Ingredients:

- 2 C. fresh spinach
- 1 medium avocado, peeled, pitted and chopped roughly
- 2 scoops unsweetened vegan protein powder
- 3 tbsp. maple syrup
- 2 tbsp. fresh lemon juice
- 1 C. milk
- ¼ C. ice cubes

Instructions:

1. In a high-speed blender, place all ingredients and pulse until creamy.
2. Pour into 2 serving bowls and serve immediately with your favorite topping.

Nutrition Information:
Calories per serving: 471; Carbohydrates: 36.2g; Protein: 32.2g; Fat: 23.5g; Sugar: 24.3g; Sodium: 357mg; Fiber: 8g

71 – Quickest Breakfast Porridge

Serves: 4
Cooking Time: 4 minutes
Preparation Time: 10 minutes

Ingredients:
- 2 C. milk
- 3 large apples, peeled, cored and grated
- ½ tsp. vanilla extract
- Pinch of ground cinnamon
- 1 banana, peeled and sliced
- ½ small apple, cored and sliced

Instructions:
1. In a large pan, add the milk, grated apples, vanilla extract and cinnamon and mix well.
2. Place the pan over medium-low heat and cook for about 3-4 minutes, stirring occasionally.
3. Transfer the porridge into the serving bowls.
4. Top with the banana and apple slices and serve.

Nutrition Information:
Calories per serving: 194; Carbohydrates: 40.9g; Protein: 5.9g; Fat: 3g; Sugar: 30g; Sodium: 60mg; Fiber: 6g

72 – Halloween Morning Oatmeal

Serves: 2
Cooking Time: 2 minutes
Preparation Time: 10 minutes

Ingredients:
- 2 C. hot water
- 1/3 C. pumpkin puree
- 1/3 C. rolled oats
- 1 tsp. ground cinnamon
- 1 tsp. ground ginger
- ¼ tsp. ground nutmeg
- 2 scoops unsweetened vanilla vegan protein powder
- 1 tbsp. maple syrup
- 1 small banana, peeled and sliced

Instructions:
1. In a microwave-safe bowl, place water, pumpkin puree, oats, chia seeds and spices and mix well.
2. Microwave on High for about 2 minutes.
3. Remove the bowl of oatmeal from the microwave and stir in the protein powder and maple syrup.
4. Top with banana slices and serve immediately.

Nutrition Information:
Calories per serving: 268; Carbohydrates: 34.4g; Protein: 28.4g; Fat: 2.4g; Sugar: 14.8g; Sodium: 269mg; Fiber: 5g

73 – Authentic Bulgur Porridge

Serves: 2
Cooking Time: 15 minutes
Preparation Time: 10 minutes

Ingredients:
- 2/3 C. milk
- 1/3 C. bulgur, rinsed
- Pinch of salt
- 1 ripe banana, peeled and mashed
- 1 large apple, peeled, cored and chopped

Instructions:
1. In a pan, add the soy milk, bulgur and salt over medium-high heat and bring to a boil.
2. Reduce the heat to low and simmer for about 10 minutes.
3. Remove the pan of bulgur from heat and immediately, stir in the mashed banana.
4. Serve warm with the topping of chopped apple.

Nutrition Information:
Calories per serving: 231; Carbohydrates: 50.6g; Protein: 6.5g; Fat: 2.4g; Sugar: 22.6g; Sodium: 121mg; Fiber: 8.5g

74 – 2-Grains Porridge

Serves: 3
Cooking Time: 20 minutes
Preparation Time: 10 minutes

Ingredients:
- 2 C. milk
- 2 C. water
- 1 C. old-fashioned oats
- 1/3 C. dried quinoa, rinsed
- 3 tbsp. maple syrup
- ½ tsp. vanilla extract
- 1 large banana, peeled and sliced
- 1 small apple, peeled, cored and chopped

Instructions:
1. In a pan, mix together all the ingredients except for banana and apple over medium heat and bring to a gentle boil.
2. Cook for about 20 minutes, stirring occasionally.
3. Remove from the heat and serve warm with the garnishing of banana and apple.

Nutrition Information:
Calories per serving: 384; Carbohydrates: 72g; Protein: 12.2g; Fat: 6.5g; Sugar: 32.9g; Sodium: 87mg; Fiber: 7g

75 – Savory Crepes

Serves: 4
Cooking Time: 20 minutes
Preparation Time: 10 minutes

Ingredients:
- 1¼ C. chickpea flour
- 1½ C. water
- ¼ tsp. red chili powder
- Salt, as required

Instructions:
1. In a blender, add all the ingredients and pulse until well combined.
2. Heat a lightly greased nonstick skillet over medium-high heat.
3. Add the desired amount of the mixture and tilt the pan to spread it evenly.
4. Cook for about 3 minutes.
5. Carefully, flip the crepe and cook for about 1-2 minutes.
6. Repeat with the remaining mixture.
7. Serve warm.

Nutrition Information:
Calories per serving: 229; Carbohydrates: 38.1g; Protein: 12.1g; Fat: 3.8g; Sugar: 6.7g; Sodium: 55mg; Fiber: 11g

76 – Egg-Free Omelet

Serves: 4
Cooking Time: 12 minutes
Preparation Time: 15 minutes

Ingredients:
- 1 C. chickpea flour
- ¼ tsp. ground turmeric
- ¼ tsp. red chili powder
- Pinch of ground cumin
- Pinch of sea salt
- 1½-2 C. water
- 1 medium onion, chopped finely
- 2 medium tomatoes, chopped finely
- 2 tbsp. fresh cilantro, chopped
- 2 tbsp. olive oil, divided

Instructions:
1. In a large bowl, add the flour, spices, and salt and mix well.
2. Slowly, add the water and mix until well combined.
3. Fold in the onion, tomatoes and cilantro.
4. In a large non-stick frying pan, heat ½ tbsp. of the oil over medium heat.
5. Add ½ of the tomato mixture and tilt the pan to spread it.
6. Cook for about 5-7 minutes.
7. Place the remaining oil over the "omelet" and carefully flip it over.
8. Cook for about 4-5 minutes or until golden brown.
9. Repeat with the remaining mixture.

Nutrition Information:
Calories per serving: 267; Carbohydrates: 35.7g; Protein: 10.6g; Fat: 10.3g; Sugar: 8.3g; Sodium: 86mg; Fiber: 10.2g

77 – Summer Treat Salad

Serves: 4
Preparation Time: 15 minutes

Ingredients:
- 2 large avocados, peeled, pitted and chopped
- 1 large apple, peeled, pitted and chopped
- 1 large peach, peeled, pitted and chopped
- 1 C. cantaloupe, peeled and chopped
- 1 shallot, chopped finely
- 1 seedless cucumber, peeled and chopped
- ¼ C. fresh lime juice
- ¼ C. fresh mint, chopped
- 6 C. lettuce leaves, torn

Instructions:
1. In a large salad bowl, add all the ingredients and toss to coat well.
2. Set aside for at least 10-20 minutes before serving.

Nutrition Information:
Calories per serving: 262; Carbohydrates: 28.7g; Protein: 3.7g; Fat: 17.1g; Sugar: 14.9g; Sodium: 20mg; Fiber: 9.5g

78 – Secretly Amazing Salad

Serves: 6
Cooking Time: 35 minutes
Preparation Time: 15 minutes

Ingredients:
For Lentils:
- 4 C. water
- 2 C. dried green lentils, rinsed
- 2 large garlic cloves, halved lengthwise
- 2 tbsp. olive oil

For Dressing:
- 1 garlic clove, minced
- ¼ C. fresh lemon juice
- 2 tbsp. olive oil
- 1 tsp. maple syrup
- 1 tsp. Dijon mustard
- Salt and freshly ground black pepper, to taste

For Salad:
- 1½ (15-oz.) cans chickpeas, rinsed and drained
- 2 large avocados, peeled, pitted and chopped
- 2 C. radishes, trimmed and sliced
- ¼ C. fresh mint leaves, chopped

Instructions:
1. For lentils: in a medium pot, add all ingredients over medium-high heat and bring to a boil.
2. Reduce the heat to low and simmer for about 25-35 minutes or until the lentils are cooked through and tender.
3. Drain the lentils and discard the garlic cloves.
4. For dressing: add all ingredients in a small bowl and beat until well combined.
5. In a large serving bowl, add lentils, chickpeas, radishes, avocados and mint and mix.
6. Add the dressing and toss to coat well.
7. Serve immediately.

Nutrition Information:
Calories per serving: 561; Carbohydrates: 66.4g; Protein: 24.9g; Fat: 22.2g; Sugar: 3.2g; Sodium: 96mg; Fiber: 29.2g

79 – Crowd Pleasing Salad

Serves: 5
Preparation Time: 15 minutes

Ingredients:
- 2 C. cooked quinoa
- 2 C. canned red kidney beans, rinsed and drained
- 5 C. fresh baby spinach
- ¼ C. tomatoes, peeled, seeded and chopped
- ¼ C. fresh dill, chopped
- ¼ C. fresh parsley, chopped
- 3 tbsp. fresh lemon juice
- Salt and freshly ground black pepper, to taste

Instructions:
1. In a large bowl, add all the ingredients and toss to coat well.
2. Serve immediately.

Nutrition Information:
Calories per serving: 354; Carbohydrates: 62.7g; Protein: 16.6g; Fat: 4.8g; Sugar: 2.5g; Sodium: 331mg; Fiber: 11.5g

80 – South Western Salad

Serves: 6
Preparation Time: 20 minutes

Ingredients:
For Dressing:
- 2 tbsp. fresh lime juice
- 2 tbsp. maple syrup
- 1 tbsp. Dijon mustard
- ½ tsp. ground cumin
- 1 tsp. garlic powder
- Salt and freshly ground black pepper, to taste
- ¼ C. extra-virgin olive oil

For Salad:
- 2 C. fresh mango, peeled, pitted and cubed
- 2 tbsp. fresh lime juice, divided
- 2 avocados, peeled, pitted and cubed
- Pinch of salt
- 1 C. cooked quinoa
- 2 (14-oz.) cans black beans, rinsed and drained
- 1 small red onion, chopped
- ½ C. fresh cilantro, chopped
- 6 C. romaine lettuce, shredded

Instructions:
1. For dressing: in a blender, add all the ingredients except oil and pulse until well combined.
2. While the motor is running, gradually add the oil and pulse until smooth.
3. For salad: in a bowl, add the mango and 1 tbsp. of lime juice and toss to coat well.
4. In another bowl, add the avocado, a pinch of salt and remaining lime juice and toss to coat well.
5. In a large serving bowl, add the mango, avocado and remaining salad ingredients and mix.
6. Place the dressing and toss to coat well.
7. Serve immediately.

Nutrition Information:
Calories per serving: 555; Carbohydrates: 71.5g; Protein: 18.1g; Fat: 24.4g; Sugar: 13g; Sodium: 69mg; Fiber: 19.7g

81 – Great Luncheon Salad

Serves: 4
Cooking Time: 5 minutes
Preparation Time: 20 minutes

Ingredients:
For Salad:
- ½ C. homemade vegetable broth
- ½ C. couscous
- 3 C. canned red kidney beans, rinsed and drained
- 2 large tomatoes, peeled, seeded and chopped
- 5 C. fresh spinach, torn

For Dressing:
- 1 garlic clove, minced
- 2 tbsp. shallots, minced
- 2 tsp. lemon zest, grated finely
- ¼ C. fresh lemon juice
- 2 tbsp. extra-virgin olive oil
- Salt and freshly ground black pepper, to taste

Instructions:
1. In a pan, add the broth over medium heat and bring to a boil.
2. Add the couscous and stir to combine.
3. Cover the pan and immediately remove from the heat.
4. Set aside, covered for about 5-10 minutes or until all the liquid is absorbed.
5. For salad: in a large serving bowl, add the couscous and remaining ingredients and stir to combine.
6. For dressing: in another small bowl, add all the ingredients and beat until well combined.
7. Pour the dressing over salad and gently toss to coat well.
8. Serve immediately.

Nutrition Information:
Calories per serving: 341; Carbohydrates: 53.2g; Protein: 15.7g; Fat: 8.5g; Sugar: 6.6g; Sodium: 670mg; Fiber: 13.5g

82 – Flavors Powerhouse Lunch Meal

Serves: 2
Preparation Time: 15 minutes

Ingredients:
- 1 large avocado
- 1¼ C. cooked chickpeas
- ¼ C. celery stalks, chopped
- 1 scallion (greed part), sliced
- 1 small garlic clove, minced
- 1½ tbsp. fresh lemon juice
- ½ tsp. olive oil
- Salt and freshly ground black pepper, to taste
- 1 tbsp. fresh cilantro, chopped

Instructions:
1. Cut the avocado in half and then remove the pit.
2. With a spoon, scoop out the flesh from each avocado half.
3. Then, cut half of the avocado flesh in equal-sized cubes.
4. In a large bowl, add avocado cubes and remaining ingredients except for sunflower seeds and cilantro and toss to coat well.
5. Stuff each avocado half with chickpeas mixture evenly.
6. Serve immediately with the garnishing of cilantro.

Nutrition Information:
Calories per serving: 403; Carbohydrates: 0g; Protein: 9.8g; Fat: 22.6g; Sugar: 1.1g; Sodium: 546mg; Fiber: 13.8g

83 – Eye-Catching Sweet Potato Boats

Serves: 2
Cooking Time: 40 minutes
Preparation Time: 20 minutes

Ingredients:
For Sweet Potatoes:
- 1 large sweet potato, halved lengthwise
- ½ tbsp. olive oil
- Salt and freshly ground black pepper, to taste

For Filling:
- ½ tbsp. olive oil
- 1/3 C. canned chickpeas, rinsed and drained
- 1 tsp. curry powder
- 1/8 tsp. garlic powder
- 1/3 C. cooked quinoa
- Salt and freshly ground black pepper, to taste
- 1 tsp. fresh lime juice
- 1 tsp. fresh cilantro, chopped

Instructions:
1. Preheat the oven to 375 degrees F.
2. Rub each sweet potato half with oil evenly.
3. Arrange the sweet potato halves onto a baking sheet, cut side down and sprinkle with salt and black pepper.
4. Bake for about 40 minutes or until sweet potato becomes tender.
5. Meanwhile, for filling: in a skillet, heat the oil over medium heat and cook the chickpeas, curry powder and garlic powder for about 6-8 minutes, stirring frequently.
6. Stir in the cooked quinoa, salt and black pepper and remove from the heat.
7. Remove from the oven and arrange each sweet potato halves onto a plate.
8. With a fork, fluff the flesh of each half slightly.
9. Place chickpeas mixture in each half and drizzle with lime juice
10. Serve immediately with the garnishing of cilantro and sesame seeds.

Nutrition Information:
Calories per serving: 286; Carbohydrates: 43g; Protein: 8.2g; Fat: 9.7g; Sugar: 6.6g; Sodium: 175mg; Fiber: 8g

84 – Mexican Enchiladas

Serves: 8
Cooking Time: 20 minutes
Preparation Time: 15 minutes

Ingredients:
- 1 (14-oz.) can red beans, drained, rinsed and mashed
- 2 C. cheddar cheese, grated
- 2 C. tomato sauce
- ½ C. onion, chopped
- ¼ C. black olives, pitted and sliced
- 2 tsp. garlic salt
- 8 whole-wheat tortillas

Instructions:
1. Preheat the oven to 350 degrees F.
2. In a medium bowl, add the mashed beans, cheese, 1 C. of tomato sauce, onions, olives and garlic salt and mix well.
3. Place about 1/3 C. of the bean mixture along center of each tortilla.
4. Roll up each tortilla and place enchiladas in large baking dish.
5. Place the remaining tomato sauce on top of the filled tortillas.
6. Bake for about 15-20 minutes.
7. Serve warm.

Nutrition Information:
Calories per serving: 358; Carbohydrates: 46.2g; Protein: 20.6g; Fat: 11.2g; Sugar: 4.5g; Sodium: 550mg; Fiber: 10.3g

85 – Unique Banana Curry

Serves: 3
Cooking Time: 15 minutes
Preparation Time: 15 minutes

Ingredients:
- 2 tbsp. olive oil
- 2 yellow onions, chopped
- 8 garlic cloves, minced
- 2 tbsp. curry powder
- 1 tbsp. ground ginger
- 1 tbsp. ground cumin
- 1 tsp. ground turmeric
- 1 tsp. ground cinnamon
- 1 tsp. red chili powder
- Salt and freshly ground black pepper, to taste
- 2/3 C. plain yogurt
- 1 C. tomato puree
- 2 bananas, peeled and sliced
- 3 tomatoes, peeled, seeded and chopped finely

Instructions:
1. In a large pan, heat the oil over medium heat and sauté onion for about 4-5 minutes.
2. Add the garlic, curry powder and spices and sauté for about 1 minute.
3. Add the yogurt and tomato sauce and bring to a gentle boil.
4. Stir in the bananas and simmer for about 3 minutes.
5. Stir in the tomatoes and simmer for about 1-2 minutes.
6. Remove from the heat and serve hot.

Nutrition Information:
Calories per serving: 318; Carbohydrates: 49.7g; Protein: 9g; Fat: 12.2g; Sugar: 24.2g; Sodium: 138mg; Fiber: 9.5g

86 – Vegan-Friendly Platter

Serves: 4
Cooking Time: 30 minutes
Preparation Time: 10 minutes

Ingredients:
- 1 tbsp. olive oil
- 2 small onions, chopped
- 5 garlic cloves, chopped finely
- 1 tsp. of dried oregano
- 1 tsp. ground cumin
- ½ tsp. ground ginger
- Salt and freshly ground black pepper, to taste
- 2 cups tomatoes, peeled, seeded and chopped
- 2 (13½-oz.) cans black beans, rinsed and drained
- ½ C. homemade vegetable broth

Instructions:
1. In a pan, heat the olive oil over medium heat and cook the onion for about 5-7 minutes, stirring frequently.
2. Add the garlic, oregano, spices, salt and black pepper and cook for about 1 minute.
3. Add the tomatoes and cook for about 1-2 minutes.
4. Add in the beans and broth and bring to a boil.
5. Reduce the heat to medium-low and simmer, covered for about 15 minutes.
6. Serve hot.

Nutrition Information:
Calories per serving: 327; Carbohydrates: 54.1g; Protein: 19.1g; Fat: 5.1g; Sugar: 4g; Sodium: 595mg; Fiber: 18.8g

87 – Armenian Style Chickpeas

Serves: 4
Cooking Time: 15 minutes
Preparation Time: 15 minutes

Ingredients:
- 2 tbsp. olive oil
- 1 medium yellow onion, chopped
- 4 garlic cloves, minced
- 1 tsp. dried thyme, crushed
- 1 tsp. dried oregano, crushed
- ½ tsp. paprika
- 1 C. tomato, chopped finely
- 2½ C. canned chickpeas, rinsed and drained
- 5 C. Swiss chard, chopped
- 2 tbsp. water
- 2 tbsp. fresh lemon juice
- Salt and freshly ground black pepper, to taste
- 3 tbsp. fresh basil, chopped

Instructions:
1. In a skillet, heat the olive oil over medium heat and sauté the onion for about 6-8 minutes.
2. Add the garlic, herbs and paprika and sauté for about 1 minute.
3. Add the Swiss chard and 2 tbsp. water and cook for about 2-3 minutes.
4. Add the tomatoes and chickpeas and cook for about 2-3 minutes.
5. Add in the lemon juice, salt and black pepper and remove from the heat.
6. Serve hot with the garnishing of basil.

Nutrition Information:
Calories per serving: 260; Carbohydrates: 34g; Protein: 12g; Fat: 8.6g; Sugar: 3.1g; Sodium: 178mg; Fiber: 9g

88 – Protein-Packed Soup

Serves: 8
Cooking Time: 1 hour 10 minutes
Preparation Time: 15 minutes

Ingredients:
- 2 tbsp. olive oil
- 1½ lb. ground turkey
- Salt and freshly ground black pepper, to taste
- 1 large carrot, peeled and chopped
- 1 large celery stalk, chopped
- 1 large onion, chopped
- 6 garlic cloves, chopped
- 1 tsp. dried rosemary
- 1 tsp. dried oregano
- 2 large potatoes, peeled and chopped
- 8-9 C. chicken bone broth
- 4-5 C. tomatoes, peeled, seeded and chopped
- 2 C. dry lentils
- ¼ C. fresh parsley, chopped

Instructions:
1. In a large soup pan, heat the olive oil over medium-high heat and cook the turkey for about 5 minutes or until browned.
2. With a slotted spoon, transfer the turkey into a bowl and set aside.
3. In the same pan, add the carrot, celery onion, garlic and dried herbs over medium heat and cook for about 5 minutes.
4. Add the potatoes and cook for about 4-5 minutes.
5. Add the cooked turkey, tomatoes and broth and bring to a boil over high heat.
6. Reduce the heat to low and cook, covered for about 10 minutes.
7. Add the lentils and cook, covered for about 40 minutes.
8. Stir in black pepper and remove from the heat.
9. Serve hot with the garnishing of parsley.

Nutrition Information:
Calories per serving: 485; Carbohydrates: 44.6g; Protein: 43g; Fat: 16.5g; Sugar: 8.5g; Sodium: 452mg; Fiber: 16.6g

89 – One-Pot Dinner Soup

Serves: 4
Cooking Time: 50 minutes
Preparation Time: 15 minutes

Ingredients:
- 1 tbsp. olive oil
- 1 C. yellow onion, chopped
- ½ C. carrots, peeled and chopped
- ½ C. celery, chopped
- 2 garlic cloves, minced
- 4 C. homemade vegetable broth
- 2½ C. sweet potatoes, peeled and chopped
- 1 C. red lentils, rinsed
- 1½ tbsp. fresh lemon juice
- Salt and freshly ground black pepper, to taste
- 2 tbsp. fresh cilantro, chopped

Instructions:
1. In a large Dutch oven, heat the oil over medium heat and sauté the onion, carrot and celery for about 5-7 minutes.
2. Add the garlic and sauté for about 1 minute.
3. Add the sweet potatoes and cook for about 1-2 minutes.
4. Add in the broth and bring to a boil.
5. Reduce the heat to low and simmer, covered for about 5 minutes.
6. Stir in the red lentils and gain bring to a boil over medium-high heat.
7. Reduce the heat to low and simmer, covered for about 25-30 minutes or until desired doneness.
8. Stir in the lemon juice, salt and black pepper and remove from the heat.
9. Serve hot with the garnishing of cilantro.

Nutrition Information:
Calories per serving: 471; Carbohydrates: 61g; Protein: 19,3g; Fat: 5.6g; Sugar: 4.4g; Sodium: 836mg; Fiber: 19.7g

90 – 3-Beans Soup

Serves: 12
Cooking Time: 45 minutes
Preparation Time: 15 minutes

Ingredients:
- ¼ C. olive oil
- 1 large onion, chopped
- 1 large sweet potato, peeled and cubed
- 3 carrots, peeled and chopped
- 3 celery stalks, chopped
- 3 garlic cloves, minced
- 2 tsp. dried thyme, crushed
- 1 tbsp. red chili powder
- 1 tbsp. ground cumin
- 4 large tomatoes, peeled, seeded and chopped finely
- 2 (16-oz.) cans great Northern beans, rinsed and drained
- 2 (15¼-oz.) cans red kidney beans, rinsed and drained
- 1 (15-oz.) can black beans, drained and rinsed
- 12 C. homemade vegetable broth
- 1 C. fresh cilantro, chopped
- Salt and freshly ground black pepper, to taste

Instructions:
1. In a Dutch oven, heat the oil over medium heat and sauté the onion, sweet potato, carrot and celery for about 6-8 minutes.
2. Add the garlic, thyme, chili powder and cumin and sauté for about 1 minute.
3. Add in the tomatoes and cook for about 2-3 minutes.
4. Add the beans and broth and bring to a boil over medium-high heat.
5. Cover the pan with lid and cook for about 25-30 minutes.
6. Stir in the cilantro and remove from heat.
7. Serve hot.

Nutrition Information:
Calories per serving: 411; Carbohydrates: 69.7g; Protein: 22.7g; Fat: 5.7g; Sugar: 7.1g; Sodium: 931mg; Fiber: 18.9g

91 – Heavenly Tasty Stew

Serves: 6
Cooking Time: 35 minutes
Preparation Time: 15 minutes

Ingredients:
- ¼ C. olive oil
- 1 large yellow onion, chopped
- 8 oz. fresh shiitake mushrooms, sliced
- 2 large tomatoes, chopped
- 2 tbsp. garlic, chopped finely
- 2 bay leaves
- 2 tbsp. mixed Italian herbs (rosemary, thyme, basil), chopped
- 1 tsp. cayenne pepper
- 4 C. homemade vegetable broth
- 2 tbsp. apple cider vinegar
- 1 C. whole-wheat fusilli pasta
- 1/3 C. nutritional yeast
- 8 oz. fresh collard greens
- 1 (15-oz.) can cannellini beans, drained and rinsed
- Salt and freshly ground black pepper, to taste

Instructions:
1. In a large pan, heat the oil over medium heat and sauté the onion, mushrooms, potato and tomato for about 4-5 minutes.
2. Add the garlic, bay leaves, herbs and cayenne pepper and sauté for about 1 minute.
3. Add the broth and bring to a boil.
4. Stir in the vinegar, pasta and nutritional yeast and again bring to a boil.
5. Reduce the heat to medium-low and simmer, covered for about 20 minutes.
6. Uncover and stir in the greens and beans.
7. Simmer for about 4-5 minutes.
8. Stir in the salt and black pepper and remove from the heat.
9. Serve hot.

Nutrition Information:
Calories per serving: 314; Carbohydrates: 46g; Protein: 14.4g; Fat: 10g; Sugar: 6.2g; Sodium: 489mg; Fiber: 12.3g

92 – Thanksgiving Dinner Chili

Serves: 6
Cooking Time: 45 minutes
Preparation Time: 15 minutes

Ingredients:
- 2 tbsp. olive oil
- 1 red bell pepper, seeded and chopped
- 1 onion, chopped
- 2 garlic cloves, chopped
- 1 lb. lean ground turkey
- 2 C. water
- 3 C. tomatoes, chopped finely
- 1 tsp. ground cumin
- ½ tsp. ground cinnamon
- 1 (15-oz.) can red kidney beans, rinsed and drained
- 1 (15-oz.) cans black beans, rinsed and drained
- ¼ C. scallion greens, chopped

Instructions:
1. In a large Dutch oven, heat the olive oil over medium-low heat and sauté bell pepper, onion and garlic for about 5 minutes.
2. Add the turkey and cook for about 5-6 minutes, breaking up the chunks with a wooden spoon.
3. Add the water, tomatoes and spices and bring to a boil over high heat.
4. Reduce the heat to medium-low and stir in beans and corn.
5. Simmer, covered for about 30 minutes, stirring occasionally.
6. Serve hot with the topping of scallion greens.

Nutrition Information:
Calories per serving: 366; Carbohydrates: 40.6g; Protein: 28.7g; Fat: 11.2g; Sugar: 4.5g; Sodium: 100mg; Fiber: 13.4g

93 – Meatless Monday Chili

Serves: 4
Cooking Time: 1 hour 25 minutes
Preparation Time: 15 minutes

Ingredients:
- 2 tbsp. avocado oil
- 1 medium onion, chopped
- 1 carrot, peeled and chopped
- 1 small bell pepper, seeded and chopped
- 1 lb. fresh mushrooms, sliced
- 2 garlic cloves, minced
- 2 tsp. dried oregano
- 1 tbsp. red chili powder
- 1 tbsp. ground cumin
- Salt and freshly ground black pepper, to taste
- 8 oz. canned red kidney beans, rinsed and drained
- 8 oz. canned white kidney beans, rinsed and drained
- 2 C. tomatoes, peeled, seeded and chopped finely
- 1½ C. homemade vegetable broth

Instructions:
1. In a large Dutch oven, heat the oil over medium-low heat and cook the onions, carrot and bell pepper for about 10 minutes, stirring frequently.
2. Increase the heat to medium-high.
3. Stir in the mushrooms and garlic and cook for about 5-6 minutes, stirring frequently.
4. Add the oregano, spices, salt and black pepper and cook for about chili 1-2 minutes.
5. Stir in the beans, tomatoes and broth and bring to a boil.
6. Reduce the heat to low and simmer, covered for about 1 hour, stirring occasionally.
7. Serve hot.

Nutrition Information:
Calories per serving: 346; Carbohydrates: 59.9g; Protein: 23.4g; Fat:3.7g; Sugar: 10.5g; Sodium: 545mg; Fiber: 16.7g

94 – Beans Trio Chili

Serves: 6
Cooking Time: 1 hour
Preparation Time: 15 minutes

Ingredients:
- 2 tbsp. olive oil
- 1 green bell pepper, seeded and chopped
- 2 celery stalks, chopped
- 1 scallion, chopped
- 3 garlic cloves, minced
- 1 tsp. dried oregano, crushed
- 1 tbsp. red chili powder
- 2 tsp. ground cumin
- 1 tsp. red pepper flakes, crushed
- 1 tsp. ground turmeric
- 1 tsp. onion powder
- 1 tsp. garlic powder
- Salt and freshly ground black pepper, to taste
- 4½ C. tomatoes, peeled, seeded and chopped finely
- 4 C. water
- 1 (16-oz.) can red kidney beans, rinsed and drained
- 1 (16-oz.) can cannellini beans, rinsed and drained
- ½ of (16-oz.) can black beans, rinsed and drained

Instructions:
1. In a large pan, heat the oil over medium heat and cook the bell peppers, celery, scallion and garlic for about 8-10 minutes, stirring frequently.
2. Add the oregano, spices, salt, black pepper, tomatoes and water and bring to a boil.
3. Simmer for about 20 minutes.
4. Stir in the beans and simmer for about 30 minutes.
5. Serve hot.

Nutrition Information:
Calories per serving: 342; Carbohydrates: 56g; Protein: 20.3g; Fat: 6.1g; Sugar: 6g; Sodium: 79mg; Fiber: 21.3g

95 – Staple Vegan Curry

Serves: 6
Cooking Time: 40 minutes
Preparation Time: 15 minutes

Ingredients:
- 10 oz. whole-wheat pasta
- 1 tbsp. vegetable oil
- 1 medium white onion, chopped
- 3 garlic cloves, minced
- 1 tsp. dried basil, crushed
- 1 tbsp. curry powder
- ¼ tsp. red pepper flakes, crushed
- 2 lb. ripe tomatoes, peeled, seeded and chopped
- 4 C. cauliflower, cut into bite-sized pieces
- 1 medium red bell pepper, seeded and sliced thinly
- 1 C. water
- 1 (15-oz.) can chickpeas, drained and rinsed
- 1 C. fresh baby spinach
- ¼ C. fresh parsley, chopped
- Salt, to taste

Instructions:
1. In a pan of the salted boiling water, add the pasta and cook for about 8-10 minutes or according to package's directions.
2. Drain the pasta well and set aside.
3. Heat the oil in a large cast-iron skillet over medium heat and sauté the onion for about 4-5 minutes.
4. Add the garlic, basil, curry powder and red pepper flakes and sauté for about 1 minute.
5. Stir in the tomatoes, cauliflower, bell pepper and water and bring to a gentle boil.
6. Reduce the heat to medium-low and simmer, covered for about 15-20 minutes.
7. Stir in the chickpeas and cook for about 5 minutes.
8. Add the spinach and cook for about 3-4 minutes.
9. Stir in the pasta and remove from the heat.
10. Serve hot.

Nutrition Information:
Calories per serving: 338; Carbohydrates: 58.4g; Protein: 15.1g; Fat: 5.9g; Sugar: 10.9g; Sodium: 80mg; Fiber: 10.3g

96 – Fragrant Vegetarian Curry

Serves: 8
Cooking Time: 1½ hours
Preparation Time: 15 minutes

Ingredients:
- 8 C. water
- ½ tsp. ground turmeric
- 1 C. brown lentils
- 1 C. red lentils
- 1 tbsp. olive oil
- 1 large white onion, chopped
- 3 garlic cloves, minced
- 2 large tomatoes, peeled, seeded and chopped
- 1½ tbsp. curry powder
- ¼ tsp. ground cloves
- 2 tsp. ground cumin
- 3 carrots, peeled and chopped
- 3 C. pumpkin, peeled, seeded and cubed into 1-inch size
- 1 granny smith apple, cored and chopped
- 2 C. fresh spinach, chopped
- Salt and freshly ground black pepper, to taste

Instructions:
1. In a large pan, add the water, turmeric and lentils over high heat and bring to a boil.
2. Reduce the heat to medium-low and simmer, covered for about 30 minutes.
3. Drain the lentils, reserving 2½ C. of the cooking liquid.
4. Meanwhile, in another large pan, heat the oil over medium heat and sauté the onion for about 2-3 minutes.
5. Add in the garlic and sauté for about 1 minute.
6. Add the tomatoes and cook for about 5 minutes.
7. Stir in the curry powder and spices and cook for about 1 minute.
8. Add the carrots, potatoes, pumpkin, cooked lentils and reserved cooking liquid and bring to a gentle boil.
9. Reduce the heat to medium-low and simmer, covered for about 40-45 minutes or until desired doneness of the vegetables.
10. Stir in the apple and spinach and simmer for about 15 minutes.
11. Stir in the salt and black pepper and remove from the heat.
12. Serve hot.

Nutrition Information: Calories per serving: 263; Carbohydrates: 47g; Protein: 14.7g; Fat: 2.9g; Sugar: 9.7g; Sodium: 53mg; Fiber: 20g

97 – Omega-3 Rich Dinner Meal

Serves: 4
Cooking Time: 40 minutes
Preparation Time: 15 minutes

Ingredients:
For Lentils:
- ½ lb. French green lentils
- 2 tbsp. extra-virgin olive oil
- 2 C. yellow onions, chopped
- 2 C. scallions, chopped
- 1 tsp. fresh parsley, chopped
- Salt and freshly ground black pepper, to taste
- 1 tbsp. garlic, minced

- 1½ C. carrots, peeled and chopped
- 1½ C. celery stalks, chopped
- 1 large tomato, peeled, seeded and crushed finely
- 1½ C. chicken bone broth
- 2 tbsp. balsamic vinegar

For Salmon:
- 2 (8-oz.) skinless salmon fillets
- 2 tbsp. extra-virgin olive oil

- Salt and freshly ground black pepper, to taste

Instructions:
1. Ina heat-proof bowl, soak the lentils in boiling water for 15 minutes.
2. Drain the lentils completely.
3. In a Dutch oven, heat the oil in over medium heat and cook the onions, scallions, parsley, salt and black pepper for about 10 minutes, stirring frequently.
4. Add the garlic and cook for about 2 more minutes.
5. Add the drained lentils, carrots, celery, crushed tomato and broth and bring to a boil.
6. Reduce the heat to low and simmer, covered for about 20-25 minutes.
7. Stir in the vinegar, salt and black pepper and remove from the heat.
8. Meanwhile, for salmon: preheat your oven to 450 degrees F.
9. Rub the salmon fillets with oil and then, season with salt and black pepper generously.
10. Heat an oven-proof sauté pan over medium heat and cook the salmon fillets for about 2minutes, without stirring.
11. Flip the fillets and immediately transfer the pan into the oven.
12. Bake for about 5-7 minutes or until desired doneness of salmon.
13. Remove from the oven and place the salmon fillets onto a cutting board.
14. Cut each fillet into 2 portions.
15. Divide the lentil mixture onto serving plates and top each with 1 salmon fillet.
16. Serve hot.

Nutrition Information:
Calories per serving: 707; Carbohydrates: 50.2g; Protein: 16.1g; Fat: 29.8g; Sugar: 7.9g; Sodium: 496mg; Fiber: 16.2g

98 – Weekend Dinner Casserole

Serves: 6　　　　　　　　　　　　　　　Cooking Time: 1 hour
Preparation Time: 20 minutes

Ingredients:
- 2½ C. water, divided
- 1 C. red lentils
- ½ C. wild rice
- 1 tsp. olive oil
- 1 small onion, chopped
- 3 garlic cloves, minced
- 1/3 C. zucchini, peeled, seeded and chopped
- 1/3 C. carrot, peeled and chopped
- 1/3 C. celery stalk, chopped
- 1 large tomato, peeled, seeded and chopped
- 8 oz. tomato sauce
- 1 tsp. ground cumin
- 1 tsp. dried oregano, crushed
- 1 tsp. dried basil, crushed
- Salt and freshly ground black pepper, to taste

Instructions:
1. In a pan, add 1 C. of the water and rice over medium-high heat and bring to a rolling boil.
2. Reduce the heat to low and simmer, covered for about 20 minutes.
3. Meanwhile, in another pan, add the remaining water and lentils over medium heat and bring to a rolling boil.
4. Reduce the heat to low and simmer, covered for about 15 minutes.
5. Transfer the cooked rice and lentils into a casserole dish and set aside.
6. Preheat your oven to 350 degrees F.
7. Heat the oil in a large skillet over medium heat and sauté the onion and garlic for about 4-5 minutes.
8. Add the zucchini, carrot, celery, tomato and tomato paste and cook for about 4-5 minutes.
9. Stir in the cumin, herbs, salt and black pepper and remove from the heat.
10. Transfer the vegetable mixture into the casserole dish with rice and lentils and stir to combine.
11. Bake for about 30 minutes.
12. Remove from the heat and set aside for about 5 minutes.
13. Cut into equal-sized 6 pieces and serve.**Nutrition Information:** Calories per serving: 192; Carbohydrates: 34.5g; Protein: 11.3g; Fat: 1.5g; Sugar: 3.9g; Sodium: 239mg; Fiber: 12g

99 – Family Dinner Pilaf

Serves: 4
Cooking Time: 1 hour
Preparation Time: 15 minutes

Ingredients:
- 2 tbsp. olive oil
- 2 garlic cloves, minced
- 2 C. fresh mushrooms, sliced
- 1¼ C. brown rice, rinsed
- 2 C. homemade vegetable broth
- Salt and freshly ground black pepper, to taste
- 1 red bell pepper, seeded and chopped
- 4 scallions, chopped
- 1 (16-oz.) can red kidney beans, drained and rinsed
- 2 tbsp. fresh parsley, chopped

Instructions:
1. In a large pan, heat the oil over medium heat and sauté the onion for about 4-5 minutes.
2. Add the garlic and mushrooms and cook about 5-6 minutes.
3. Stir in the rice and cook for about 1-2 minutes, stirring continuously.
4. Stir in the broth, salt and black pepper and bring to a boil.
5. Reduce the heat to low and simmer, covered for about 35 minutes, stirring occasionally.
6. Add in the bell pepper and beans and cook for about 5-10 minutes or until all the liquid is absorbed.
7. Serve hot with the garnishing of parsley.

Nutrition Information:
Calories per serving: 463; Carbohydrates: 76.7g; Protein: 18.5g; Fat: 10.1g; Sugar: 3.2g; Sodium: 431mg; Fiber: 11.6g

100 – Meat-Free Bolognese Pasta

Serves: 5
Cooking Time: 2 hours
Preparation Time: 20 minutes

Ingredients:
For Bolognese Sauce:

- 5 tbsp. olive oil, divided
- 3 celery stalks, chopped finely
- 1 medium carrot, peeled and chopped finely
- 1 medium onion, chopped finely
- 1 C. quinoa, rinsed
- 3 C. fresh mushrooms, chopped
- 4 garlic cloves, chopped
- ¾ tsp. dried oregano
- ½ tsp. dried thyme
- ¼ tsp. dried rosemary
- ¼ tsp. dried sage
- 1/8 tsp. red pepper flakes
- 1½ C. homemade vegetable broth
- 2 cups tomatoes, peeled, seeded and crushed finely
- ½-1 C. water
- 1 tbsp. balsamic vinegar
- 4 bay leaves
- 2 tbsp. nutritional yeast
- ¼ C. oat milk
- Salt and freshly ground black pepper, to taste
- ¼ C. fresh basil leaves

For Pasta:

- ¾ lb. whole-wheat pasta (of your choice)

Instructions:

1. Preheat your oven to 300 degrees F.
2. In a large Dutch oven, heat 3 tbsp. of the olive oil over medium heat and cook the celery, carrots and onion for about 10 minutes, stirring frequently.
3. Stir in the quinoa and cook for about 3 minutes.
4. Add the remaining oil and mushrooms and stir to combine.
5. Increase the heat to medium-high and cook for about 5 minutes.
6. Add the garlic, dried herbs and red pepper flakes and cook for about 1-2 minutes.
7. Add the broth and cook for about 5 minutes.
8. Add the tomatoes, water, vinegar and bay leaves and bring to a boil.
9. Remove the Dutch oven from heat and transfer into the oven.
10. Bake, uncovered for about 1½ hours, stirring once after 1 hour.
11. Meanwhile, in a pan of the lightly salted boiling water, cook the pasta for about 8-10 minutes or according to package's instructions.
12. Drin the pasta well.
13. Remove the Dutch oven from oven and stir in the nutritional yeast and oat milk.
14. Divide the pasta onto serving plates and top with Bolognese sauce.
15. Garnish with basil leaves and serve.

Nutrition Information:
Calories per serving: 510; Carbohydrates: 71g; Protein: 17.1g; Fat: 18.3g; Sugar: 5.9g; Sodium: 241mg; Fiber: 6.5g

CPSIA information can be obtained
at www.ICGtesting.com
Printed in the USA
BVHW050408291221
625048BV00005B/1007